BR

AND

MALTA
THE STORY
OF AN ERA

JOSEPH ATTARD

Publishers Enterprises Group (PEG) Ltd

Publishers Enterprises Group (PEG) Ltd
P.E.G. Building, UB7, Industrial Estate,
San Gwann SGN 09, Malta.

First Edition 1988
Reprinted 1995

ISBN: 99909-0-058-2

Photoset and printed in Malta by P.E.G. Ltd.

By the same author

In English
I Chased a Ghost
Oleanders in the Wind
The Battle of Malta
The Ghosts of Malta
Industrial Relations in Malta

In Maltese
It-Toroq Kollha jwasslu għal Ruma (All Roads lead to Rome)
Taħt is-Sinjal ta' Taurus (Under the Sign of Taurus)
Ix-Xitan wasal fit-Tlettax (The Devil came on the Thirteenth)
L-Aħħar Appuntament (The Last Appointment)

CONTENTS

LIST OF ILLUSTRATIONS

FOREWORD

The history of Malta had always been dominated by the periods of the island's occupation by foreign powers. Phoenicians, Carthaginians, Romans, Arabs, Normans, Angevines, Castillians, Knights of St. John and the British. The list seems interminable; with every period having left its indelible marks for posterity on the country's characteristics. It can be said however that in both historical and human terms, none of the first eight periods was as moving, interesting and pregnant with meaning and definition of the Maltese character as the last one, when Malta was a British colony.

The era of British presence was moving and interesting because of mercurial fate that fluctuated during those hurrying years of change, all wrought with trials and triumphs, hardship and benevolence, anguish and heroism. The same times then having been full of meaning because they were characterized with the continuous endeavours of the Maltese to emerge from their long history of feudalism which generated the beginning and development of politics, as well as their love for freedom and democracy, largely helped along by the British. The era then became even more interesting since it had as a background some of the upheavals on the other side of the fence as British statesmen could visualize the imperial destinies of Britain with the rise and fall of her empire and grandeur.

This period of British presence can also be seen as a long and rational struggle for ideals between friends, interspersed only by times when Britain and Malta were in danger. As they were during the three wars that raged during this era. Such occasions always brought unification. Then when the dangers were over, both nations would continue with the struggle which never stopped until the Maltese asked for and Britain acquiesced to have the island become independent, and eventually a Republic.

I would never be so bold to claim to have written all there is to be said about this era. There had been so much happening, that doing this would have been a mammoth task. Indeed it is only now that the wealth of documents and despatches relating to those years is being properly sorted out and placed in some order. However, going through what is available with an unbiassed mind, and the faithful scope of research one cannot fail to discern a steady and magnificent story which conforms with my conviction that history should not be written just to establish the facts, but to rationalize their truths. It is also a narrative which brings out the fact that as with history itself, the story of Britain and Malta has no beginning and no end. It has only a meaning which transcends an era of sharing with the British nation a common love of freedom, common political thought and common memories. It is indeed more of a meaning that had contributed to Malta's past glories, as it is now bolstering her future as an independent republic in a shaky world.

Much of the material for this work was gathered by myself in the course of time, and I don't exclude the possibility that some sources of information might have been blurred from recollection to be properly acknowledged. But I cannot fail to mention Dr. Vincent Depasquale who always answered my questions with a wealth of information. Then I must record my recourse to the books *British Malta*, Books I & II by A.V. Laferla (A.C. Aquilina & Co.), and *The Story of Malta,* by Brian Blouet (Faber & Faber, London) on which I had to draw for information. Both these works, and to a lesser extent others that I have appropriately listed in the bibliography afforded me useful insights into details that had perforce to go into my story.

Such work had also to carry illustrations and I want to express my thanks and appreciation to Mr. John Sultana of the National Library of Malta and his staff at the Palace Archives for having provided me with the pictures I wanted. I am also indebted to the National War Museum Association of Malta, *The Times* and Independent Print for affording me the use of photographs from their collections.

I have imposed a pattern of my own on the story I have written. Aimed to reach the general reader more than the historian. In the final analysis it is a story of Maltese toil and endeavour which made the Maltese nation, with the collaboration of the British co-protagonists. It would therefore be a fitting tribute to dedicate this book to the peoples of the two nations.

Malta   Joseph Attard
February, 1988

CHAPTER I

THE NEW DAWN

Malta, 1st April 1979. The morning was still, with a touch of wind as the thin mist which had been pearling the countryside was lifting. Fields and gardens were now uncovered, full of blossom, multi-coloured and with sweet-smelling flames as if called out by the spring sun. The air was full of song from the morning thrushes and there was the crowing from late cocks from yards and middens. But otherwise silence reigned supreme. Nothing, and no one moved in what had become ghost towns and villages seemingly emptied of their inhabitants to leave only an echoing shell.

In contrast the Grand Harbour was from the early hours of that morning as busy as a beehive. The main aisle scintillating ~~in the~~ morning sun and the creeks and inlets that bite everywhere into the harbour's periphery were full of boats. Big and small, crowded with people carrying small red and white Maltese flags and also Union Jacks. All were converging on to the centre for the important event of the day. There had been a whole week of celebrations which had reached the climax on the previous day, the 31st March, 1979. In the morning the last British troops to serve at Malta, 130 marines of the Salerno Company had marched to their point of embarkation at Vittoriosa, meaningly followed by a sole ex-serviceman who on his own initiative had marched with them. Then they embarked on the RFA logistic ship *Sir Lancelot* and departed for home. The RFA ship *Tarbatness* had followed suit in the afternoon, while the last of a long

1

series of RAF VC-10 flights took off from Luqa airfield ferrying the last RAF personnel from the island to the United Kingdom. In the evening then there had been the climax on the specially erected monument with a ceremonial lowering of the last Union Jack signifying the end of the 179 year British military presence in Malta.

The thousands of people who had attended those ceremonies and who could not take to a boat on the morning of April 1st were lining the high wind swept ramparts around the harbour. But the air of high purpose they had taken with them which moments before could be sensed through their clamour was now suddenly curbed and lost in the profound silence that ensued. For long moments there was an air of desolation falling on that otherwise noisy harbour, as if all were observing a few minutes of silence for a departing friend. The spell was broken by a ripple of murmuring moving amongst the crowds, and the sound of a solitary aircraft approaching from the direction of Luqa Airport which drew all eyes to the sky. A lone Nimrod of the RAF then came in low, seemingly making a heavy going in consonance with the similarily heavy hearts of the thousands watching it from below. At one stage, its pilot Air Commodore H.D. Hall, the last Air Commander in Malta tipped the aircraft to starboard to salute the crowds and the President of Malta Dr Anton Buttigieg who was amongst them. A thousand voices then broke into delirious shouting, and hands waved or clapped. By the time they stopped the Nimrod had already set course for England.

It was now the turn of HMS London to bring the curtain down. She sailed majestically across the Harbour, that had for 179 years hosted and sheltered her many ancestors, with the band of the Royal Marines filling the air with a moving march, and escorted by launches of the Armed Forces of Malta and hundreds of decorated boats. On its bridge there was Admiral Cecil waving to the crowds, with his wife and 13 year old son Robert. The crowds waved back, but their shouting soon broke down to give way to tears from heavy hearts. As the ship went past the breakwater she fired a 21 gun salute to be acknowledged by a counter reply from Fort St Elmo. Then the crowds fell back into silence as the ship faded into the mist laden horizon leaving only its wake to seal the end of an era.

★ ★ ★

As fate would have it this date marked the anniversary of another occasion 266 years before when Malta was having one of her frequent flirtations with Britain. "The English nation has always availed itself of our port," had written Grandmaster Perellos of the Order of St John to Queen Anne on that day, "and her admirals and ambassadors have always received the honours due to the generals and ministers of such a powerful and florid kingdom." The grandmaster was referring to the times when the British fleet was allowed the use of the Maltese harbour and also provided with munitions during the Tripolitan war.

This was the time of aristocratic Malta well past the worst part of her troubled history in subjugation to Phoenicians, Carthaginians, Romans, Arabs, Normans, Angevines and Castillians. It was now a Malta of the Knights of St John who had taken over in 1530, and from an arid sparsely populated rock with only a harbour dominated by the magnificent Fort St Angelo, and the two towns of Birgu and Mdina the old capital had been transformed into a gem of civilisation. The Knights had not only built towns and villages to be endowed with their auberges and palatial buildings but also erected superb systems of fortifications which went down in history as the most impressive monuments in Europe of Western military architecture of the sixteenth, seventeenth and early eighteenth centuries. The Maltese had found scope to exploit their belief and love of democracy but their sober character had come out in the open during the Great Siege of 1565 when they rallied to back their rulers against the Infidel that invaded their land. They had endured the hardships of battle for four months until the enemy was driven away. From then onwards however a series of Grandmasters and Knights of the various langues had tied with each other to embellish the island. The old town of Birgu became a city to be re-named Vittoriosa in memory of its fight and victory over the Turks. Other towns rose up from the dust and more churches, aqueducts and lordly gardens found their place in the landscape. Substantial forts began to ring the coast, with watch towers as characteristic of their epoch as the Martello Towers in the south coast of England were of theirs. The sumptuous taste of the Knights was however to be best reflected in the city of Valletta which took the name of the Grandmaster who built it and was made, as it still is, the island's capital.

The Knights had also during their two and a half centuries occupation brought culture to Malta where there is still to be seen the heritage of great artists like Caravaggio, Mateo Perez d'Alecio, Paladini, Leonello Spada, Giuseppe Mazzuoli, Mattia Preti and Favray, all imported by the Order and who can be said to have brought the glories of the Renaissance to Malta. Under these masters then there were neutral Maltese artists and craftsmen who were second to none and whose traditions have only lately died out. Throughout this time the power of the Order and the prestige of its navy grew as fast as the power of Islam waned. Its vessels policed the Mediterranean seeking out corsairs and pirates, collecting Muslim slaves and setting free Christian captives in the process, and the weight of gold in ransom swelled the Order's treasury.

It is no wonder then that Britain looked on Malta with benign eyes. There were of course the occasions when feelings were ruffled and relations tended to become strained. Such as in the time of George II when the Grandmaster, then Pinto de Fonseca had reason to complain of the high handedness of English captains who chased and captured French ships within the territorial waters of Malta. There was also in 1764 the annoying behaviour of Dodsworth, the English consul who was a thorn in the Order's side. When Dodsworth was imprisoned there arose a diplomatic incident which brought a British protest. But it was as always the English sovereign who went out of his way to soothe the Knights' ruffled feelings, and relations continued to be friendly, with British ships being allowed to use Maltese harbours.

More than simple friends one could say Britain and Malta were something closer. So much so that when the French revolution broke out and the Order's property in

4

France was seized, Britain offered compensation to the grandmaster at the time, Emanuel de Rohan Polduc on the one condition however that he would help in the war against France. Indeed, notwithstanding the victories of the French Army in Italy which suggested prudence and neutrality to the Order there were 482 Maltese sailors recruited for the British fleet which was beseiging Toulon, while the harbour and dockyard of Malta were offered for use by the British Admiral Hood.

There was nothing to indicate that Malta would ever have to be conquered by the British, and her people mindful of their glorious history were always particularly sensitive to any such suggestion then, as they are indeed now. It was only fate that gave Malta to Britain. And it had to be a British blunder to spark it.

After languishing for years in possession of Gibraltar, occupied in 1704, and having Minorca restored to her by France in 1763 when the seven years war had come to an end, Britain lost this island again to a combined Spanish and French army in 1782. An attempt to hold to Toulon eleven years later had failed and this left her with only Gibraltar, right at the Western end of a Mediterranean infested with the strong fleets of Genoa and Venice, and plagued by the endemic coastal raiding by sons of the Ottoman, another empire still to be reckoned with. It soon became imperative for Britain to look for some other foothold, and eyes turned towards Corsica. British forces landed on this island on 7 February 1794, but it took them up to 10 August to take full possession.

Britain had produced a lot of plans for Corsica. A dock and fortifications that would have secured the island from any attack. None of which had materialised, however. It was now that Napoleon Bonaparte began building an armada at Toulon, Marseilles and Genoa. But strangely enough what British preparations were made for any eventuality must have been only in the way of guessing Bonaparte's intention. An invasion of England was being mentioned, while there were also expectations of a strike against Ireland or Portugal. It could also be Sicily or Corfu. Why not? And the guessing continued with a mounting tension which however was not strong enough to keep the Pitt government from recalling British troops from Corsica which were needed elsewhere. This was until now a bad decision; but it became a blatant blunder when it was decided to evacuate Corsica altogether. And while British forces were still in process of embarkation, Bonaparte's troops began moving in during October 1796.

It might have then looked as if this had been the French general's intention all along. But it wasn't. He had somewhere else in mind and had waited only not to tempt faith and get involved with the British. As things turned out they played into his hands, and with his mind set at ease with the occupation of Corsica, he set out with his armade on 8th May 1788. It was a force of thirteen sail-of-the line, eight frigates plus two Venetian 64 gun ships with six other frigates and other smaller craft. Seventy two naval ships in all, which were to be joined by 400 transports carrying some 36,000 troops. The rendezvous was made on the 19th, and the whole force got under way generating more guessing about its destination.

It was on 9th June that Bonaparte had his first look at the impressive battlements of Malta which was to be his first prey.

The precision in attitude of the Knights had long succumbed to the inevitable change that so often takes place in human institutions, and the Order had kept declining through soft living and lassitude throughout the reign of fourteen grandmasters. There had been those of them who had tried to bring it back on its feet but without success. In 1797 the last grandmaster to attempt reviving the lost *raison d'etre*, Emanuel de Rohan Polduc, died, and with the Order having by now come close in becoming an anachronism the Knights elected the German Ferdinand Joseph von Hompesch. He was an ill choice since he had already been accused of having betrayed the institution he was being called upon to rule. But whether this was true or not he was also a classic example of craven incapacity and worse. He was also weak and irresolute as no other grandmaster had been before and he was certainly not fitted, neither by character nor temperament to cope with the responsibilities he had been ready to assume. And much less to confront Bonaparte on that day of 9th June 1798.

The first cue to the drama that was to be enacted came from the Frendh general on the following morning when he requested permission to enter Grand Harbour and take on water. However weak, the Grandmaster was not that stupid, and only granted permission for the French to send in four ships at a time. This was the kind of reply Bonaparte wanted. "Water is refused," he exclaimed, "so we will go and take it." And that was that. Had Hompesch the men and will to resist it would still have been impossible for him to do it, because unknown to him there had already been put some troublemakers ashore and contact made with the French Knights. Collaboration was also assured from the Officers commanding the artillery and fortifications, as well as from the Order's senior engineer Toussard. So what should have been an attack was nothing more than a walk over. There was some resistance in the sister island of Gozo where the troublemakers had not penetrated, and Maltese batteries opened fire on Bonaparte's men as they landed while 2300 men gave battle. But by darkness all defence crumbled in front of the French Grenadiers who had penetrated everywhere.

That night the Maltese Islands became a French possession. In six days' time then, Bonaparte had converted them into an imitation of a Department of the French Republic with everyone being ordered to wear the blue, white and red cockade, and streets being given French names. He was equally efficient in despoiling the country which was then a storehouse of gold and silver, and precious stones. While all this was going on the Grandmaster and all but the oldest and feeblest of the Knights left Malta and scattered. Some went to Trieste; others to St Petersburg where they sought protection from Emperor Paul. But the Maltese were left alone and unaided. From now on they had to fend for themselves.

Bonaparte left Malta after a few days leaving a garrison of 3053 infantrymen and five companies of artillery to police the island. As Commander-in-Chief he left General Vaubois. But the fervour for freedom and democracy with which the Maltese were imbued did not allow them to stay idle. The seed of revolt was generated and there was no lack of patriots to come forward and plot to overthrow their oppressors. There were priests and lawyers, doctors and businessmen, as well as many others from all walks of life. The spirit of rebellion was running high with everyone and there was soon formed an undercover National Assembly. There were selected three leaders, a priest Canon Francesco Saverio Caruana, a businessman Vincenzo Borg and a public notary Emmanuele Vitali. In a few months they had mustered some 3200 men whom they could ill equip with guns; another 7000 had to be satisfied with pikes and cudgeols. This motley army was ready to bide time for the insurrection, but there was trouble brewing when on 2nd September two Maltese lawyers were assigned the duty by the French to auction the Church property in the outskirts of the city of Mdina. The people objected, and when the lawyers ran for safety they were soon hemmed in by a throng of villagers. A french Captain Masson who was the commander of the garrison there intervened brandishing a sword, and struck a small boy. This was the limit for the crowd who chased the French officer into a nearby house, to be caught and thrown through a window without much ado. The soldiers of the garrison sensing trouble quickly shut the city gates and tried to work out some sort of surrender, but one of them foolishly fired his musket, and that was that. The crowd stormed the place and butchered the whole of them. The word quickly went round and the Maltese, armed or not were soon chasing the French out of every town and village, until those that managed to save their skin were penned down in Valletta and the three cities of Vittoriosa, Cospicua and Senglea.

The first stage of the insurrection had brought them what was considered a resounding victory, but the resurgents knew they could not stop there. If they were to throw the French out they had to persist, but they could not do this unless they had more arms and provisions. They thought immediately of asking for this help from King Ferdinand of Naples and the Two Sicilies. But even if their request were to be granted and reinforcements be sent, there was nothing to keep the French from being similarly reinforced. Unless there was some fleet to blockade Malta and prevent this. It was here they thought of Britain, with her powerful fleet in the Mediterranean. So two delegates from the National Assembly, Luigi Briffa and Francesco Farrugia were quickly put on a vessel and sent to Naples to see King Ferdinand. With them, however, they also carried a letter addressed to Admiral Horatio Nelson asking for help with the blockade.

Indeed, none knew that Nelson had neither the mind nor the force to afford such help. Because while they were enacting this part of Maltese history he had just written another glorious page in the annals of British naval history by fighting and defeating Bonaparte in the Battle of the Nile. He had sunk most of the French ships at Aboukir, amongst them Bonaparte's flagship *L'Orient* which was carrying the loot taken from Malta then valued at £240,000 which was a considerable sum in those days. And his ships had not escaped unscathed. So much so that as the vessel carrying the Maltese delegates was on its way to Naples, the tired and depressed British Admiral was also returning there with his battered fleet. Then fate or Providence made him come across the small vessel off the coast of Sicily.

The Maltese sailors hailed the British flagship *Vanguard* and they were soon taken aboard to the admiral to tell him of all that had happened at Malta and to give him the letter they had for him. There is no doubt that Nelson was moved by what he learned. It was inconceivable even to him how a small people as the Maltese were, abandoned by the Knights in their hour of need could have risen with such success against their mighty oppressors. He wanted to help Malta, and promised to do so, but first he had to re-organise his battered fleet. He was well aware, however, that he couldn't very well delay his support if this were to have any effect. So he decided that until British ships could be despatched to blockade the French he would ask his allies the Portugese to stand in. Indeed the Portugese fleet was soon off Malta to be joined soon after on the 17th September by Captain Saumarez who was returning with booty captured at the Battle of the Nile out of which he dispensed with 1062 muskets and ammunition to the Maltese. As if this was not enough Nelson wanted to have British presence felt in the undertaking, and finding he could spare some ships after all he sent one of his Aboukir heroes, Captain Alexander Ball, to Malta with his ship *HMS Alexander*, accompanied by a frigate, a sloop and a fire-ship. On 12th October the combined British and Portugese fleets were sealing the island and the French. Twelve days later Nelson himself arrived in Malta. He spent six days there, most of which were devoted to discussing the situation with Captain Ball and the Maltese leaders who were charmed by his affability and interest in Malta's situation.

This visit afforded him the chance to verify that what food supplies had been promised to be sent to Malta by King Ferdinand had indeed not arrived. There was also the question of Gozo, which, lightly defended as it was by the French could be occupied. Captain Ball landed there with a small force on 28th October and was followed by Captain Cresswell and a contingent of marines who attacked and captured Fort Chambray. For the first time ever the Union Jack was hoisted on the ramparts of Gozo.

Malta was, however, a different problem. The French were known to have had a good supply of corn as well as the mills to grind it. To substitute normal water from the aqueduct which was cut off they had a lot of wells to turn to. With their guns on the ramparts openely masked they did not seem to have been keen for conflict, but none was misled to think they were unwary. As the new year drew on it became distressingly obvious that it wasn't going to be easy to dislodge the French from their position without more visible assistance than surreptitious subsidies and food. What the island wanted were arms and troops. Then as if to throw coal on slowly dying fires through despondency after months of inaction, Nelson dispensed of the Portuguese fleet and left only the British squadron to continue with the blockade under the charge of Captain Alexander Ball. None understood this move, and it might have reduced many of the Maltese stalwarts for freedom to the depths of depression. After all, it was common knowledge that the French were only biding their time to bring in reinforcements and supplies. Then they would attack and there was not much hope of holding them. It became suddenly imperative to have something done and the Maltese knew that they had to do it themselves.

Notwithstanding the odds against them they tried to go through the French lines into Valletta hoping to take the city by stealth. But they failed, and their leader, a pious and brave priest Father Michael Xerri together with 44 others were captured and shot.

This was a heavy blow to morale. But there was soon to be a more special sense of foreboding with the news that followed of the capture of Naples by the French and the fleeing of the Royal family to Palermo. It dawned on everyone now that any hope of keeping Bonaparte away would be futile. The only alternative was to place Malta under the protection of some strong nation, and with the kingdom of Naples and the Two Sicilies now impotent there was only Britain to qualify. This realisation brought immediate repercussions and determination, and the Neapolitan King was on 9 February supplicated to agree to the British being asked to afford special protection to Malta and also to have the British flag hoisted there. This was refused, and heads became hot to lend to tiffs and arguments which even the prevailing sense of unity was not strong enough to override. Those who kept their heads, however, went straight to Nelson under the pretence of asking him to send Captain Ball ashore to try and pacify the dissensions that had cropped up. But more than this they urged him to take Malta under British protection.

It was not an easy request. And an unorthodox one. But what might have looked like a voluntary surrender of individual liberty was indeed a national loyalty to a supranational ideal. The request embodied too, the concept of love for freedom of which Britain was the image of at that time. And Nelson consented, on Britain's behalf, to afford this protection, even if it was to be only for the duration of the war. As a sign of his good faith he asked to have the Sicilian flag raised together with the British colours. Peace was in sight for Maltese minds and there was much rejoicing. Even as the French were triumphing again in Italy, which if anything, made this arrangement more pressing.

It was then that there was the unexpected arrival in the Mediterranean of the French Admiral Brui which called for Nelson to drive him out. This necessitated the use of most of the British fleet which on 13 May 1799 withdrew the blockading warships, as if in repetition of the Corsican blunder.

Malta was stunned, and all seemed to be lost. The all conquering French had only to capture Sicily to cut off the only source of supply. But as if this was not enough, Czar Paul of St Petersburg who had been declared Grandmaster of the Order of St John after sheltering the Knights that had escaped from Malta was now offering to send troops. This might have looked as a godsend, but the Maltese were more alarmed at the possibility of having the Order back in Malta. It had during the last years of its presence become for them a little less hateful than the French. There was indeed much perturbation. But the French left them no time to think about it for emulating what had been done at Corsica they now emerged from their besieged positions to lay hands on all remaining Maltese vessels and supplies, and to blockade harbours.

Indeed this might have been a blessing in disguise since it made Nelson realise his error which was on the verge to losing him the initiative. This made him despatch four warships to resume the blockade, again under the command of Captain Ball whom, the now more hard pressed King Ferdinand of Naples, agreed to confirm as Governor of Malta.

It was a historic *contra-temps* which sent the Maltese into delirious joy. A similarly infected Britain and typically wise when all is almost lost followed up with determination. Nelson moved two regiments from Minorca to Malta, together with General Graham. They arrived in Malta on the *Northumberland* and the *Culloden* on 9 December 1799. It now became touch and go; a race against time before Bonaparte would attack, rather than to see which of the two sides in Malta would starve first. Graham's first action was to press for more troops and with 1200 Russian soldiers offered by Czar Paul being unable to cross over for lack of means, Nelson soon arranged to have them ferried over. There was also a Neapolitan contingent brought over, but it was still considered that this was not enough.

Nothing of this must have been lost to the French and

they too tried to reinforce their besieged garrison in anticipation for what they could expect from the hurried British build up. An intrepid attempt was made with a naval squadron which comprised troopships with 4000 men and a storeship to try and break the blockade only to be foiled by Nelson who captured the lot. Maltese morale soared again, now at a time when General Graham had decided to fill up the blanks in his desired force with Maltese. He had only to suggest this to them, and they rose like one man to join the newly formed regiment of Maltese Light Infantry *I Cacciatori di Malta* in June 1800.

This was timely since Bonaparte had by now completed his triumphs in Italy and was looking to Sicily as his next prey which would bring him closer to Malta. With the local build up complete the time factor had shifted. It was now not as much which side will starve first as to whether the besieged French will hold on until Bonaparte could strike.

The situation might have deteriorated with the British command in the Mediterranean changing hands. But fortunately enough the new Commander-in-Chief, Sir Ralph Abercomby, must have been imbued with the explosive nature of the situation. With his taking over he immediately sent Major-General (later Sir Henry) Pigot to take over command from Graham. With him he sent also two additional regiments which reached Malta on 18 July. To assess the situation better, then Abercromby followed them to Malta himself. But if he had expected to find a rosy situation he must have been very much disappointed.

He found the Maltese troops who were to be the backbone of his army were still desperatly short of food. Moreover, they had throughout the long time of this crisis been receiving only half pay. Morale was at its lowest ebb and there was certainly no more enthusiasm for combat. To make matters worse this state of feeling had spread all over the population similarly hit by disease and an epidemic which had already by then claimed 20,000 lives.

Fortunately the position of the besieged French was no better. A desperate attempt from their part to take back and use two warships, the *Justice* and *Diana* which were in their possession after they had escaped from the Battle of the Nile possibly to bring relief or to get out, failed. Both ships were captured by the British. It now became evident for them that it was profitless to resist. So they capitulated on 2nd September 1800, two years to the day from the Maltese uprising.

It took three days for the formalities of the capitulation to be sorted out, with the French insisting that no Maltese should be allowed to enter Valletta until they were gone, and with having a mixed Anglo-French guard to see to this. But if there were tiffs they were only of pique, and they had spread over to the British as well – between Pigot and Ball. But they were not allowed to jeopardise the French surrender which was concluded.

Captain Ball's day arrived when he drove into Valletta in state, accompanied by Maltese dignitaries and representatives of the Maltese bodies that had contributed to that occasion. As the French left, the Maltese people converged on Valletta and St John's Church where Archbishop Labini intoned the *Te Deum*. On the roofs of all public buildings for the first time ever, the Union Jack was flying in the brisk September breeze. Signifying the dawn of a new era.

CHAPTER II

BIRTH OF THE COLONY

The British found in Malta a very challenging situation. The outlook of the first people they had to confront was very promising. Looks, dress and behaviour were of the best. They were the elite of the spearhead of a hosting nation who had in a way copied and taken to the Knights' way of life. They lived in big houses. Not very comfortable maybe, with vast rooms all communicated with each other, but otherwise decorated with leather curtains and hanging arras. Their domestic habits too, were organized on knightly patterns. They made their own clothes and had their particular recreations. Some of them even carried titles of nobility awarded to them by the Order of St John.

But behind them there was the mass. Hard pressed by poverty, disease and illiteracy. Now somewhat palliated by new hopes for the newly gained freedom. They made a very impressive picture of a feudal society and an anachronism that had survived only through their staunch resistance evolved through centuries of old and constant domination by allien powers. Their resistance throughout the ages, moving down from generation to another had been sustained by a stubborn sense of clan loyalty, strengthened by their love for democracy and blessed by the shooting but iron hand of Mother Church. These were the direct descendants of forefathers who when held in subjection by an oligarchy in the pay of foreign overlords had united in revolt, and followed their bishops and their priests in both peaceful protests and in armed insurrection. They were indeed the same people who had starved the

15

French into submission and kicked them out. So, notwith-standing their humble outlook, what principles of democracy, freedom and equality of opportunity they had, were not something to be imported with the new British Parliamentary system they were hoping to get.

A Maltese language was spoken by all the sections of the population. It had, however, not yet secured the status of a written language. Where writing was involved, Italian was used, being the language of the kingdom of the Two Sicilies to which Malta belonged. Italian was therefore the official language of the Courts of Law as well as the Church. This was also subjugated to the Kings of the Two Sicilies by virtues of the fact that its bishops had to be nominated by them for eventual appointment by the Pope. And obviously these were always Italian. The English language was spoken by a minority, limited to a commercial community in Valletta, no doubt learned through their contacts with crews of English merchantmen and men-of-war.

It did not take long for the point to be driven in that there was purpose and character beneath the ordinary looking individuals. If there had been disease it could have been brought by the constant shortage of water in the country. Poverty might have been the result of agricultural methods having proved to be cruelly inefficient, and illiteracy had to give way to endeavours of hard work for their meagre living. There must have been amongst them, however, the nucleus ripe for learning and culture, for Captain Ball had as one of his immediate tasks, the reopening of the University and a Jesuit College which had been suppressed by Bonaparte. And the curriculum of Latin, Italian, Arithmetic, Mathematics, Physics, Drawing, Rhetoric, Logic, Metaphysics, Dogmatic and Moral Theology, Civil and Canon Law, and the Humanities was no fluke.

The British accepted the situation that had fallen in their lap, and were set to acquisce in it. After all they were only interested in the way how the island could fit in their war operations. With her geographical location and the con-figuration of her coastline there could be established excellent anchorages. And this|in the centre of a civilized

16

world and astride the main trade routes. There was also the many installations on shore that had been built and used by the Knights. And the buildings and storehouses in Valletta and the Three Cities in the shelter of Grand Harbour. There was also a galley arsenal in one of the creeks, and a slipway with a magazine in another. Together these could form the nucleus of a dockyard and a victualling yard, with everything being secured by the line of fortifications left intact since the Knights. Only that there was a problem.

Because however positive and eligible wsa their acquisition, the British knew that Malta belonged to the Kingdom of the Two Sicilies. And even with this power unable to take over there was The Grand Priory of Russia created in 1797 with Czar Paul being elected Grand Master of the Sovereign Order, and now a strong contender for the island, egged on, no doubt, by a constant ambition of an irruption into the Mediterranean and the lifelines of the West. Britain had recognised his new status, and it was going to be hard to deny him what he considered was his due.

Now that this problem arose, it soon came out how and why Sir Charles Stuart had given up his post of Commander-in-Chief Mediterranean to be succeeded by Abercromby in the Spring of 1800. His had been a defiant refusal to agree to have Malta garrisoned conjointly by British, Russian and Neapolitan troops. And rather than submitting to superior orders he resigned his command. The man who had stood firm on this point might have been Henry Dundas, the Minister for War. But now after being softened by the first reports on Malta he had received from General Graham, he too had changed over and was in favour of holding the island. Similarly Lord Grenville, who had initially made no bones about preferring Minorca, was now coming round as well. It seemed that everyone who came in touch with the island was being charmed. Except William Pitt, the Prime Minister. With him there was still a serious doubt. And he was not an easy person to fathom. Yet, when pressed, he could not help conceding that giving away Malta would be a regrettable fact.

Fortunately enough he was never required to give a

decision, for in March 1801 his government had to bow out and he was succeeded by Adrington.

It was now Malta's turn to await anxiously the reactions of the new government. First indications were of an agreeable British parliament intending to hold to the island. To further allay local preoccupation there was the murder of Czar Paul, and with him died what expectations he had for the return of the Order of St John to Malta. The more so when his successor, Czar Alexander renounced what rights might have existed. Still, Maltese minds were not set at ease. Something else was in the air.

Whatever it was, however, did not hold Britain from consolidating her hold on Malta. The advice of Sir Ralph Abercromby was sought about laying the foundations of a future colony. Because this was how the island was being looked at now. With all the normal functions under the Knights having been continued, it was obvious to the British Commander-in-Chief that his first drive should be to establish proper administration which was totally lacking. On his advice, Captain Ball was recalled, and a Mr Charles Cameron was appointed as a Civil Commissioner in his stead. On 14th May 1801 then, Lord Hobart, the Secretary of State for War and the Colonies issued further directions for the running of administration. The post of Civil Commissioner was to be separate and additional to that of Commander of the Forces. But both holders were to act conjointly in running local affairs. The property left by the Knights was decreed to have become property of the British Crown. Civil Courts and Judges remained functioning as before, and so did the Customs and duty tariffs.

The Order of St John had in its time been spending the princely sum of £10,000 a year on the maintenance of hospitals, amongst them Lazzaretto which was described as being the most complete in the world. This was to be continued but with some effort at economising. And to make up there was an English expert on quarantine, a Mr William Eton brought over as Superintendent of Lazzaretto which he was to turn into a Quarantine establishment.

The tenor of all these directions could not but show

British determination to retain Malta and assume its sovereignity. But there persisted a silent wave of unrest amongst the Maltese. Something was worrying them. And it came out soon after. It was that same autumn to be exact when the first rumours reached Malta of British unrest and an expressed wish to cease hostilities with France. This meant Bonaparte, and he meant Malta. It had become a foregone conclusion with the Maltese that if England were to cease hostilities she would have to abandon the island. This brought a flare of consternation which no amount of British reasoning could put out. The Maltese were no fools, and true to their character, as on so many similar occasions before during their long history of feudalism, the moment of danger with a threat to national survival brought them together. Priest and peasant, noble and beggar were all suddenly miraculously united. Their first step was a representation made up by Chiefs of the villages and others who went to Charles Cameron on 19 October, 1801. They explained their case and he listened. But the picture they made was not of his doing. So a delegation was made up and went to England on 1 February, 1802.

But by now The Adrington administration was set on its course. It wanted peace at all costs and no amount of imagined fears of Bonaparte's cunning being behind the pressure that was made would deviate it. "If it is determined to withdraw British troops from Malta" said one of the clauses of the petition made by the Maltese delegation, "the people of Malta pray that they may be permitted to conduct their own affairs. The Maltese are determined not to submit to any other power than Great Britain, preferring otherwise to perish under the walls of their city if they cannot maintain their liberty and independence."

They were brave words and truly meant. But they had no effect on Britain now longing for peace. If Malta had to go in the process then let her go. And Britain gave in. The proposed peace treaty was made out. It placed Malta under the dominion of the Knights of St John. Then it was signed at Amiens on 27th March, 1802.

Hardly had the ink dried on the parchment that hell was let loose in Britain. There was sharp criticism by the Opposition in both Houses of Parliament led by Lords

Grenville and Spencer in the House of Lords and Windham in the Commons. The press came out in a vicious attack, all directed against the re-establishment of the Order of St John in Malta. They could of course not undo what had been done but they made the Adrington administration feel small under the withering scorn. British pubic opinion was all for retaining Malta. But not the government.

The official news of the signing of the peace treaty reached Malta on May 16, 1802 with HMS *Maidstone* and was publicly announced in a proclamation by Cameron. It wasn't an auspicious occasion and gave much food for thought. There had been two months of anxious expectancy. Maybe with the occasional bit of news filtering through. But always leaving hope in the confirmation that was to follow. Now that this had arrived there was no more hope. And the die was cast. Life seemed to go on as usual, with fixed routines. The general Maltese was an early riser and went to Mass daily. Thence to his work if he had any, without having to bother with any meal like what the temporary rulers called breakfast. His first meal was lunch, again a hurried affair, to be taken at home or at his place of work. Then for those who would be free there would be the afternoon siesta, since the hot weather had already set in. Wine shops would come alive in the late afternoon and evening, but at seven everyone woudl return home. Except those who had to meet and plot. And there was much to discuss and plot now. The Declaration of Rights made on 15th June, 1802 and to which all had subscribed ceased to be a piece of paper. It had now become an undertaking which must be implemented, since nothing had happened to change the situation.

But something did happen. This could be surmised two months later when Captain (now Sir) Alexander Ball unexpectedly returned to Malta. He was the same man who had always enjoyed the implicit faith of the islanders, and the mere sight of him spelt a good augur. Particularly at the the time with the British having to leave the island within a further month according to the treaty. Ball had been appointed Britain's Plenipotentiary to the Order of St John which meant that he would have to remain when the Order took over. But there must have been something else since five days after his arrival Cameron left for the United Kingdom, supposedly on leave, but never to return to Malta. It was expected that Ball would start immediately to fulfill his engagements as required by the treaty, but none knew of the emphasis made on him by Lord Hawkesbury, the Secretary of State for Foreign Affairs to see that all the conditions for the British evacuation were fully observed before he was to relinquish possession of Malta. These conditions included the election of the Grandmaster, the provision of a garrison by his Sicilian Majesty, and the guarantee of Prussia, Russia and Austria. None of these had as yet been implemented. It seemed that Britain was suspicious, and having second thoughts.

If there was an indication wanted that all was not well this came with the arrival in Malta of the French Pleni-potentiary General Vial on 18th August who lost no time in rounding up the few sympathisers of the French who had remained on the island. They were persons who had been given French titles during the occupation no doubt for the collaboration. It became obvious that Vial intended to use them to create a French party in Malta. He also tried to influence the Archbishop, at that time a Sicilian Monsignor Labini. But Ball was too shrewd for all this. He began by forbidding the wearing of any insignia of the Order. As to the rest he was not only a professional soldier and an aristocrat, but with a background which was typical of the time. His acute perception of what was being concocted made him realise that the Order of St John, already poor and without means at the time of the treaty had only just been despoiled further by Bonaparte of its revenues in Piedmont and Parma which mutilated and depauperised it still further. How could it therefore be expected to assume the ruling of an independent state in such a short time? It all came out to him, as indeed it had been realised by the Maltese themselves long before that the restoration of Malta to the Knights would be tantamount to handing it to Bonaparte and France. And this was pressed home, even as the first Neapolitan troops arrived in Malta on 8th October, 1802 in compliance with one of the conditions in the treaty.

It was a difficult situation, and maybe also the time for

the British government to be in a dilemma. But it did not take long to be resolved. Hobart, the Secretary of State for the Colonies replied to Ball by a most secret despatch on 17th October, 1802. More than a reply it was an instruction. To suspend all measures for evacuating the island of Malta, and to continue in the exercise of his duties as Civil Commissioner of the island. Britain had changed mind.

Malta was now declared to be a part of Europe. This was done in anticipation of the stationing of British troops there, who would thus not be entitled to any extra pay by virtue of the fact that the island was a European station. A declaration that served Britain at the time, but was to gain even more significance for Malta in posterior times.

Lord Hawkesbury, the Foreign Secretary had also briefed the British Ambassador in Paris in anticipation of the expected outburst by Bonaparte. Indeed this came sooner than expected in January 1803 when Lord Whitworth, the Ambassador, was asked to inform the French Government about the situation at Malta. It was Bonaparte himself who received Whitworth with tolerable cordiality but immediately burst out charging England with provoking France on many points. Mostly, however, in not evacuating Malta and Alexandria. In the tirade that followed Whitworth's diplomatic reply bringing in some of the French latest dubious actions, Bonaparte continued to say that it was in vain to speak of Piedmont and Switzerland, as they were more trifles. But he would rather put the British in possession of the heights of Monmarte than Malta.

The significance of his words was not lost. Neither on Whitworth nor on Britain. The Maltese were proved to have been right from the start after all. It was now useless for the Pope to select Chevalier Ruspoli as Grandmaster for Malta in compliance with another condition of the treaty. When this one refused there was appointed another one in his stead – Bailiff Giovanni Tommasi who sent his Lieutenant and Plenipotentiary to Malta and asked for immediate evacuation of British forces. But Ball was not to be moved. He had in the first instance advised Tommasi not to go to Malta since the people were hostile to him. Now to his plenipotentiary he said he had to await instructions from his Majesty's Government. A delaying excuse if there was one which did not delude Bonaparte, now openly seen as the one who was pulling the strings. "If, on receipt of my despatches," he thundered at the British Ambassador at the Tuileries on 13th March, 1803, "orders are not issued for the immediate surrender of Malta, then war is declared. I declare my firm resolution to see the treaty carried into effect. If England will be the first to draw the sword, then I shall be the last to sheathe it."

It had come to that. What one could call an ultimatum from the stronger than ever Bonaparte to a Britain not yet out of her rigorous extremities brought on her by the last war. There was a reply in compromise suggesting France would evacuate Holland and Switzerland while Britain woud leave Malta within ten years to be able to occupy and fortify Lampedusa. But after the ten years lapse, the island would be given to its inhabitants and be acknowledged as an independent state. But Bonaparte would not hear of this. It had to be either Malta — or war.

And Britain chose war, which was declared on 16th May, 1803.

★   ★   ★

With the resumption of hostilities there must not have been a happier man than Horatio Nelson, now appointed Commander-in-Chief Mediterranean. He took the news to Malta himself, now completely swayed by the island's strategic position. More than a haven for his ships he was seeing in it the fulcrum to a lever with which he might make the Mediterranean a British lake. From there he could watch the French at Toulon and strike whenever it became necessary at the fleet that was known to be mustering there.

He was not the only one to be lost in this kind of jubilation. Lord Hobart was soon ordering Ball to get rid of General Vial and the Neapolitan troops now that Malta's destiny seemed to have been set. And in the process appointed Ball as Civil Commissioner. This was befitting, but it was not needed to spark his exuberance. Well before he had received Hobart's instructions, Ball was already seizing all French and Ligurian ships in Harbour and ordering Vial and the Neapolitans to leave. To complete the picture there were also the people, who being more than ever before set to be entrenched in the British way of things, were not only rejoicing, but consciously feeling that what troubles and anxiety they had been through, had after all been a good price to pay for their release. As fate would have it, there was also a wind of good fortune blowing in the way of English and Italian merchants choosing Malta as a base for their trading which brought a spurt of employment to the inhabitants. But nonetheless Ball found more than 1,500 men to enlist and form two infantry battalions and a corps of artillery to start the first Maltese garrison under British rule.

He roped in also a few hundreds of veterans to swell the police force. These were soon being required to curb jubilant British sailors who had played wandering jews in the Mediterranean for too long, and which now seemed to have found a second home. They welcomed the magnificent harbours and the towns with their cute shops and sympathetic islanders. But they also went for the women. Little knowing of the strict homes and familiar life of the people, with their unselfish regard for the daughters of the house to be protected from what was regarded as dangerous contacts with foreign and amoral ways of life. A number of scuffles ensued which did no good to anybody.

Neither did these please Ball. He already knew enough of Malta and her people who divided most of their time between laying behind the familiar latticed balconies of their house and the leather *portieres* of their church doors. His only consolation was that this was the kind of worry that could be rectified quickly, and nothing to be compared with the confusion that he had found waiting him in the adminstration left by his predecessor Cameron. More than the organisation of government departments which had been left in shambles he had to see to reorganise the supply of corn which had all to be imported and the re-establishment of trading, both local and foreign. This latter being difficult through quarantine restrictions which had to be enforced because of the many epidemics that were raging in the Mediterranean. The fever which had almost depopulated Gibraltar in 1804 was one of them. But on the whole all went well and there was evident progress made in all that was known to keep a nation quiet and happy.

Maybe the quiet description should be qualified as being away from fighting and similar troubles. Since the word cannot be applied in the true sense of its meaning. Because now Malta was on the way to becoming cosmopolitan. Not only because of the many merchants but also through the motley crowd of Greeks, Albanians and Bulgarians. This to be supplemented by mercenaries of various nationalities, and also French prisoners-of-war who were being taken to be kept there. Englishmen with good intentions kept also trickling in, and one of these who was later to write many reports about this period was Samuel Taylor Coleridge. He arrived in Malta in June 1804, as a rheumatic young man of 32. He was the friend of John (later Sir) Stoddart then the King's and Admiralty Advocate who lived in a French Auberge. And that was where Coleridge went to stay. He also earned the esteem of Sir Alexander Ball who gave him an assignment as a confidential person to accompany a convoy sailing to the Black Sea to bring corn. But this was revoked in the last moments before sailing by the death of Macaulay, the Public Secretary, when Coleridge was asked to fill the vacant post. It cannot be said what might have been the effect on the career as a man of letters which Coleridge was destined to make had he remained in Malta, but with the work being uncongenial, and with his being an addict to opium he had to return to England in September 1805.

Even before then there was the very important constitutional element to be considered. Notwithstanding all there was to indicate Britain's firm intentions to retain Malta, the pecularity of the island's acquisition was never in those first years regarded strong enough to encourage the endowment of the islanders with any special rights and privileges. Indeed until 1802 there had been a British foregone conclusion that notwithstanding everything the island would eventually go back to the Order of St John. So a development of a system of self government known as *Consiglio Popolare* (Popular Council) was encouraged.

This might have been taken as a privilege, but British intentions were only to neutralize what French influence there still existed. It was only in the beginning of 1805 and the realisation of the island's position and qualities to become a fortress of Imperial defence that there began to be the first serious thoughts of consolidating Britain's possession. This suggested a change in the constitution. And the change would have been made had it not been for Bonaparte. On 18th January, 1805 his admiral Villeneuve succeeded in giving the slip to the British fleet and put to sea with his squadron. This set everyone guessing on the French intentions. Ball thought of Egypt. Others felt it would be Sicily which sent the British cabinet in a frenzy. In March, Sir James Craig was ordered to Malta with four battalions of infantry and a small detachment of cavalry and artillery to be used in protection of Sicily should this be required, but by the time they reached Malta which was on 18th July, Villeneuve was still at large keeping everyone guessing. Except Nelson. His attitude of waiting seemed to imply that he was anticipating Bonaparte's tactics. And while every power in the Mediterranean was still in the dark after nine long months of inertia, Nelson made history when he remarked: "Whatever the French may intend to do, I trust, and with confidence, that they are destined for Spithead."

But Villeneuve's action had been only a nine month feint intended to keep everyone's attentions and the British fleet in the Mediterranean. Now that the time was ripe, Bonaparte set for England and was held back only by the British last line of natural defence, which was the English channel. He turned back to the Mediterranean, which Nelson had left, pushed by a whim which had turned into an obsession.

Far from being such, it was a tactical feat. The British Commander-in-Chief met the French fleet off Cape Trafalgar and one of the biggest naval battles of the time ensued. The French fleet was smashed, and Bonaparte was defeated. French seapower was finally crushed. But Nelson was killed.

Malta missed Nelson. But his loss was a bigger blow for Ball who was now left practically alone to confront his many enemies amongst those who were supposed to be his

English friends. One of them was William Eton who had started as Superintendent of Quarantine in 1801 but had transformed himself into something different. Ball thought he had got rid of him when he left Malta for England supposedly on sick leave. But his antagonism persisted even there, where he remained for many years, with the Malta Treasury paying him his salary.

Indeed Ball was wise enough not to let such petty occurrances worry him. He must have been one of the few straight Britons of his level at the time with enough tasks to keep him busy. Because of the still uncertain occupation rights of Malta he knew now that the time had come for the anomalous situation of British constitutional rule to be regularised. He was aware this was wrought with difficulties. Not only with finding what would suit Britain and be agreeable to the Maltese, but also because there was still the Sicilian right to the island which had not yet been given up. Even after the lapse of so much time it seemed there was still a lot to be done, and with so little time to do it. The death of Monsignor Labini, the Archbishop of Malta on 30th April, 1807 gave him the chance to try and complete one important task he had been wanting to do. Since Charles V had given Malta to the Knights in 1530 it had been established that the Grandmaster had to submit names of eligible clergymen recommended for the archbishopcy to the Sicilian king who would then forward them to the Pope for selection of the archbishop. Now Ball took the bull by the horns and for the first time ever, submitted a Maltese – Monsignor Fernando Mattei. The fact that Mons. Mattei was accepted and eventually made bishop by the Consistory of 18th September, 1807 made the case for Maltese bishops. It also confirmed British intentions to maintain and protect the Roman Catholic faith in Malta which was a very important point not to be missed by the inhabitants.

Ball somehow knew his time was running short, but he had the consolation to witness an air of affluence going to the island he loved when the British navy began to blockade all French territories. This took many merchants to Malta and the British Government played up by issuing licences for export from the country to any part within the

Strait of Gibraltar as long as the merchandise was produced in any of His Majesty's dominions and carried in British or neutral vessels. So Malta became a port for transhipment. Ball had more plans but he was not to see any of them materialise. After a short but severe illness, he died on 25th October, 1809. He was laid to rest in Fort St Elmo, but a masoleum was erected to his memory in the Lower Baracca Gardens overlooking Grand Harbour, where it stands till these very days.

The choice for a successor fell on Rear-Admiral Sir Richard Godwin Keats, but ill health prevented him from taking up the appointment. So on 14th April, 1810 General Hildebrand Oakes was appointed Civil Commissioner in his stead. His was a very auspicious start since it appeared that he took on a very affluent island. Dr Charles Meryon, who had accompanied Lady Hester Stanhope, who was William Pitt's niece to Malta in the summer of 1810 had described the women of Malta in his biography of Hester Stanhope. He gave details of face, body and dress. But he also mentioned how they were fond of excessing in gold ornaments which they estimated by value more than taste. Their ears, necks and arms were stiff with rings, chains and bracelets, and they wore shoe-buckles of gold or silver. This reflects the state of Malta and her people when Oakes took over, which is as well reflected by the Commissioner's almost regal entertainments, also fabulously described by Dr Meryen. "Dinners of fifty or sixty covers were of everyday occurence at the Governor's Palace," he said, "and the singular usage of a high table, as in college halls was not uncommon at suppers after balls." But there were also troubles rising mainly from the now swelling number of French prisoners that were being taken to Malta. What worried Oakes, however, was not as much the number of those prisoners as one of them – Lucien Bonaparte, who was Napoleon's younger brother taken there on 23rd August, 1810 with his retinue of 41.

It is true that Lucien Bonaparte had not been on the best of terms with his brother, and in fact he was captured with his ship by two British frigates while he was on his way to the United States to get out of Napoleon's way. But he was still good enough to provide an excuse to his more volatile brother then riding the waves of success in Europe. The young Bonaparte complained on being treated like other prisoners by being placed in Fort Ricasoli. So a very frightened Oakes placed him in San Anton Palace which was normally used by Civil Commissioners. However, he had many sleepless nights because of this and would not rest until he could get rid of him. His appeals found response, and the younger Bonaparte was quickly conveyed to the United States.

Hardly had he got rid of him that there appeared in Malta another upstart in Lord Cochrane, the tenth Earl of Dundonald. A fiery impetuous daredevil who had distinguished himself in many a naval action attacking the French navy, and had finished in the House of Commons to denounce the navy and the Vice Admiralty Courts. His reason was that notwithstanding the numerous prizes he had captured, the extortionate fees he had to pay these courts in Malta had deprived him of compenssation for his conquests. It was after his statement was shouted down and ridiculed that he went to Malta in 1811. Hoping to find the regulation tables for the fees with which to prove himself.

Until now his visit was a normal one. But when he was refused the table he wanted by the courts, he took the law in his hands, went into the Judge's robing room, took the table he wanted from a private cupboard and left. Immediately he knew, Oakes ordered his arrest, and the news of what promised to become a *"causa celebre"* spread like wildlife. It was here that there was a turn to the dramatic when a marshal was sent to take him in. Cochrane met him with a pistol, and the court official ran away for his life. Another marshal was sent to execute what the first one had failed to do, and he too was confronted by the wild Cochrane. But instead of running away this one got police assistance. By now crowds of people who knew of what was happening were following closely to witness the outcome. This came with four burly policemen going to the Naval Commissioner's house where they found Cochrane sitting in a chair as if nothing out of the ordinary had happened. Without much ado, the policemen picked him up, chair and all, and carried him away to the town goal, to the merriment of all those who were witnessing the affair.

Had the matter ended there it would have been just another British tomfoolery to which many had become accustomed. But it was now that the dramatic turned into the burlesque when Cochrane insisted that as a distinguished prisoner he shoulkd be allowed to entertain his friends at government's expense. Oakes should have sent him packing. But he didn't. Instead, what food and drink were ordered by Cochrane were given to him, and he invited his friends from the squadron to partake of what was certainly not wardroom fare. Service and discipline were obviously being ridiculed, so Cochrane was offered bail which he refused. He made no bones about his expectations that if and when he wanted to get out, his men would pull the goal down. So to appease his vanity he was offered the chance to escape. The bars of a window were filed, and this did it. After partaking of his last banquet, Cochrane left the prison via the window, and within a short time he was on his ship and left.

It was an interlude that might not have done any good to Oakes' blood pressure. But it certainly deluded many more, seeing how every troublemaker had to be an Englishman who would invariably get away with it which to many smacked of disrespect for all that was Maltese. It certainly made it more difficult for anyone to hope for a positive response to the desire being expressed for constitutional improvements. The truth was that Oakes was hoping for this too and might even have persuaded the people to wait a little bit more, allowing time to quieten Cochrane's episode down, had it not been for the next person who materlialised to plague him and topple his applecart. This time it was William Eton again, suddenly returned from England, complete with an own formulated plan of a constitution which he was saying was bound to satisfy the people of Malta. Oakes knew immediately that this time he had a political agitator on his hands and without much ado had him sacked from the service on 11th September, 1811. Again, he should have done much more. In fact, this did not stop Eton. He had already published a book "Authentic Materials for a History of the Principality of Malta" which he was claiming described the right kind of constitution for the island. Moreover, he had already assured himself of adherents to propagate his claim. One of his followers went even as far to go the Secretary of State in London and plead Eton's case. Fortunately enough he was refused recognition as the representative of the Maltese people.

However, whatever Eton's scope might have been, the now long glowing embers of Maltese political identification were kindled into a fire. There was nothing visible to disturb everyday life. The men continued working in the dockyard and the farmers tilled their land. Maltese soldiers continued to serve and policemen kept law and order. The judges too were still dispensing justice, and civil servants kept the wheels of administration turning. Everything seemed normal. But everyone knew of the impending outburst and of the inexorable traditional Maltese will to die before yielding sacred rights to any power. Oakes knew this too. And so did Britain. That is why she acted immediately.

On 5th May, 1812 Oakes received news of the formation of a Commission under the Great Seal for an immediate inquiry to be held into matters touching the Civil Government, Law, the Judicial and other matters with a view of placing the Civil Government of Malta upon a permanent and well defined footing. There would also be more efforts to promote the interests of the people and the British Crown. The Commission was to be composed of William A. Cout who had been Charge d'Affaires at the court of Palermo, together with John Burrows, a Chief Justice of Dominica. The third member was to be Oakes himself. Indeed the two members of the Commission arrived on 20th June, and on the following day they set to work. So with their well known good faith the Maltese paused and decided to wait. After all this could be what they had been wanting. And while they waited fate smiled at them on the international front. The Russian alliance with France had collapsed and took the Czar on Britain's side. The British exploited the situation and in the draft of a treaty that followed on 18th July, 1812 made Russia declare that she was no longer interested in the restoration of Malta and the Order of St John.

The report of that Commission was never published but its contents were allowed to come out bit by bit to coincide with the economic fluctuations of the local situation. With trade and work being on the increase in that part of the year it was mentioned that the Commission had recommended the discontinuation of the system of administration by the *Consiglio Popolare*. This was good news. But instead there was to be complete authority, both civil and military vested in a Governor, who would be assisted by an advisory Council of four English and four Maltese members to be selected by him. The administration of justice was to be reformed while it was considered advisable not to change old laws. To coat the pill there was the last clause about the Roman Catholic religion being maintained and protected.

It was of course a copy of a formula that had been adopted as a basis for every British Crown Colony government which the Maltese did not want. It had been generally expected that the new type of British rule would be in some sort of a Maltese Congress with the Civil Commissioner remaining to assist. But either because they were alienated by the good timing of the issue, or because they were too stunned to speak, the people seemed to acquiesce. Diplomatically as always, Hildebrand Oakes was soon offered the post of Governor in the new set up. But being of ill-health he refused, as indeed he had already asked to be relieved as Civil Commissioner. So rather than waste precious time the Government had to look somewhere else.

It is not excluded that the cauldron of dissatisfaction was nonetheless boiling, but there was no inkling of any unrest. So that year 1813 began with good prospects for Britain. Oakes was happy too because of his impending release from a job and responsibility that were proving too heavy for him. So much so that we still have his despatch of April 1813 to the Secretary of State complimenting him on the outcome and informing him of the satisfactory situation prevailing in the island. Little did he know when he penned that despatch that it was his last to bear positive news. On 3rd May, the daughter of a shoemaker in Valletta died under strange circumstances. Soon after her mother followed. The health authorities pounced on the premises, as usual alarmed by the plague epidemic which had broken in Costantinople, Cyprus and Alexandria the previous year. They hoped that this was another false alarm like others they had had. But it wasn't. Both deaths were confirmed as having been due to the plague, and they set out to stamp it out.

But the pestilence continued to spread, mowing down life without mercy. It took hold of almost every town and village to the extent that prisoners had to be let out of jail to transport the infected and bury the dead. When local prisoners died as well there was resort to criminals being brought from Sicily. But this proved to be unsatisfactory and the Maltese had to step in themselves again. The peak was reached in July, and the government was soon on the brink of bankruptcy. In the meantime Oakes, who had been due to be relieved of his post had agreed to stay until his successor arrived, but now his health failed him and he could no longer face the strain. The British Government knew there had to be a replacement appointed. Also that he had to be a strong man in all respects. So in July 1813 there was announced the appointment of Sir Thomas Maitland as the first Governor of Malta.

Maitland, better known to those who knew him by his nickname of *King Tom* did not go to Malta straightaway on his appointment, but his fame preceded him. He was known to be a quarrelsome fellow and always spoiling for a fight. He was also a cynic giving very easily to outbursts of scorn and temper. On the other hand, he was known to have risen from nullity to a very powerful man who could face difficulties and thwart intrigues. He was moreover a good administrator and a capable and energetic public servant, with his qualities always standing him in good stead, particularly when he was with his back to the wall. He had been placed in command of the Ionian Isles in 1807 where he did a very good job. So much so that he was to retain that command even while he took over at Malta. His biographer Walter Frewen Lord had occasion later to describe him as "with one foot in Malta and the other in Corfu to bestride the Mediterranean like a Colossus".

The Governor arrived in Malta on 4th October, 1813

when the plague was still affecting the island. He went to work immediately and issued his first proclamation to characterise the image he carried. It was plain and straight-forward, expressing the king's intention to recognise the People of the Maltese Islands as subjects of the British Crown and to secure for them their religion, improve their Courts of Law with a view of meeting swifter justice, and to see to the happiness, wealth and prosperity for all. The people listened and hoped. But they did not know what to believe. The plague had wrought havoc both with their health and their enthusiasm. Maitland seemed to know this for he took strong measures to isolate those who were still stricken, using the police in the process and giving the rest the air and will to live. By December there was only one village which remained infected, and this he encircled with a wall and sentries, letting no one in or out until it was completely clean on 29th January, 1814. The first people to get his wrath were the doctors who created obstacles because of their views on the plague and its causes. But he would stand no nonsense and brought them to their knees by removing the ring leaders which made the rest play up. In his proclamation which also removed his imposed restrictions, he did not forget to declare that day as one of solemn prayer, and was all out for a Te Deum of Thanks-giving to be sung at St John's Church, in Valletta. Nobody knew by then that he himself never bothered about any religion.

It was the more ironic then when on agreeing for the Thanksgiving ceremony in St John's he was asked by the Archbishop whether he was attending and if so, whether he would sit on the throne. Maitland did not understand. But then it was explained how the Grandmasters of the Order had been authorised by the Pope to have a throne on the right of the high altar in St John's. In 1808 Alexander Ball had raised the matter, intending to have a Royal Throne to be used by the Civil Commissioner.

Maitland quickly played safe and said that he had no right to sit thereon, but he added that the throne should be kept vacant to signify His Majesty's Sovereignity in the Islands. The Archbishop concurred and erected another throne for himself on the left to keep the royal one vacant.

What Ball had not achieved with a lot of discussion, Maitland got with a hint.

As if in the way of a challenge by faith, there was another outbreak of plague in the sister island of Gozo in March, but with Maitland's energetic drive, this was quickly stamped out in a question of two months adding only another 96 dead to the 4,668 that had died in Malta.

By now it was spring, and in more ways than one. The fields were covered with the purple clover, and the bright sunlight was shimmering on the white stone. Or buildings in towns and ashlar walls in the countryside. Life had suddenly become like a lull. Broken only by the peasantry walking to its fields and hoping to achieve a miracle in the unrewarding ground. In the towns, however, the people were soon in a bustle as news were coming in. News of Bonaparte and his capitulation to the victorious allies in Paris. News of his abdiction and his transfer to the island of St Helena to be followed by the restoration of French monarchy. The climax came soon after with the Peace Treaty signed in Paris on 30th May, 1814. With a victorious Britain laying down, and the other signitories accepting, that the island of Malta and its Dependencies were to belong to full right and sovereignity of His Britannic Majesty.

There was resurrection in Malta. Of spirits and belief in a people that had again found faith in the nation they had voluntarily embraced. By the time that a year later the Congress of Vienna had set its seal upon this historic event, Malta had set hers. It was engraved in bronze on marble over the Main Guard in Valletta which had once been the Chancery of the Order, and read as follows:

MAGNAE ET INVICTAE BRITANNIAE
MELITENSIUM AMOR ET EUROPAE VOX
HAS INSULAS CONFIRMAT A.D. 1814

(To Great and Unconquered Britain
The Love of the Maltese and the Voice
of Europe. Confirms these islands. A.D. 1814)

CHAPTER III

BRITISH REFORMS

The early summer of 1815 was marked by glorious weather. More than the usual number of people began to be seen in the streets and countryside forgetting past doubts and worries in the warmth of the sun. It wasn't just the aftermath of the plague which was past and gone. But also the fever of expectation that had now gripped everyone after the island's confirmation as a British Colony. Indeed the gilded world of a British Malta seemed to be at its zenith.

For the British Government the year 1815 was the beginning of a decade of peace. But there was also unrest in the Ionian Isles and the untimely withdrawal from Pantalleria. Sicily was abandoned to the Bourbons and a high state of ferment had appeared in Greece. All of these being factors to mount up an intense diplomatic activity. But in some corner of the labyrinthine complexity of this activity there was also that little which concerned Malta.

The undisputed acquisition of the island was already being hailed as one of Britain's biggest achievements. It had also come at the right time to ensure the important naval base for her dominant fleet which was to be further strengthened in the coming years. But planning for posterity involved development, both of fortifications and garrison, and also the collaboration of the Maltese, now with their poor economic situation and also a doubt however slight of their constitutional future. There already was talk and dreams of Britain making the Maltese islands a seat of a considerable University which would attract young men from all over the Mediterranean. Also of establishing Malta as a central point of big commerce. But this was the kind of talk that did not impress anybody. Not even Maitland. He had by now an impeccable knowledge of the people, as if their character had lain open to him like a book. And the British Government did well in letting him say what was to be done.

As fate would have it, he was the man on the spot to save them from a debacle. It came when he mentioned St John's Church in one of his despatches, following a claim by the Church to make it its own.

This Church, built by Grandmaster La Cassiere between 1573 and 1578 on the design of Maltese architect Girolomo Cassar, had in its time been the Conventual Church of the Order of St John. La Cassiere's allocation of a chapel to each of the national langues of the Order had enticed the richest and most powerful houses in Europe at the time to vie with each other for the whole of 200 years to embellish their representative chapels. The priceless altar pieces and the sumptuous frescoes of the ceiling by the Calabrian painter Mattia Preti, harmonising with the Flemish tapestries with designs by Rubens invoked then, as they still do to-day, an aura of splendour. St John's was then already a jewel of Maltese heritage. More than that it was an important symbol of a nation's faith.

"That is to be considered as Government property," had replied the Secretary of State to the Governor, "but what use can we make of it?" There had then been the suggestion from someone else to have it turned into a Protestant church.

"Oh no," had replied Maitland. "You will do nothing of the sort." And the tone of his message drove the point in, with the Secretary of State replying back that the church was not on any account to be made a place of Protestant worship, but it was to be used therefrom by His Majesty's Catholic subjects. Had Maitland's advice not prevailed, the British occupation of Malta might well have had a different outcome.

Now that he was given what could be described as a free hand the intrepid governor continued to work like a bull-dozer. He reorganised the law courts, enacting a new

Constitution of the Superior Courts of Justice. There were sweeping changes in the set-up that had existed before. Judges were given fixed salaries but they had to serve at the pleasure of the Sovereign. The old *Consolato del Mare* (Maritime Consulate) was abolished and substituted by a Commercial Court with one judge and four consuls nominated by merchants to be approved by him. The Civil Court was to consist of three halls, each taking cognisance of cases according to the financial element involved. There were similar changes in the Criminal Court, but there Maitland made news when he abolished torture of any kind and the police were no longer allowed to detain persons without an accusation for any length of time. A High Court of Appeal was also instituted for both the Commercial and Civil Courts. Any cases of evident injustice and hardship could now go for redress to the Supreme Court oif Justice, which was to be presided by the Governor and to have four members, two of which were to be Maltese. Moreover, following instructions received from the Secretary of State, he laid down that the Supreme Court proceedings were to be held in English, as were to be all proclamations, in this case coupled with Italian. Because of this, the English language was to be introduced forthwith into the curriculum of lawyers, notaries and legal procurators, while all petitions addressed to government and contracts were similarly to be in that language.

None of this was that easy to introduce. There were also obstacles, particularly from judges who seemed more prone to remain anchored to the system of judical tyranny to which they had been accustomed. But there was nothing and no one to stand in Maitland's way. And the majority of the population acquisced and rejoiced in what was being done. Things seemed to be moving in the right direction leaving time and scope for personal problems to be attended to. These too might have very often been affected by the times.

The becoming of Malta as a British Colony had filled Maria with joy. She had to face much trouble from her parents after she had met George, an English sailor from HMS *Revenge*. Hers had initially been only a flirtation like many others which some Maltese girls were having with

British servicemen. But when her parents came to know of it, they became furious to the extent of threatening to banish her to a convent rather than having her respond to the amoral ways of a foreigner. Only that by now Maria was in love with George. She had found none to keep her with the problems. Neither friend or familiar. It was only her confessor who did something and asked her to pray. "God's will shall be done," he had told her. "After all the British are not barbarians." And this was what had set Ġanni, her father, thinking. He had fought the French sixteen years before and could make comparisons. He had also got a job at the dockyard which brought him in daily contact with members of George's race. And truly enough he was soon realising that they were not barbarians. As he loved his daughter he was ready to agree to her court had there not been the question of religion. Then one day, egged on by his wife, he made bold and asked George in the pidgin English he had learned at the dockyard whether he was ready to leave his protestant faith and become a Catholic.

"Why not?" said the English sailor. And that was that. Ġanni and his wife were soon thanking God for having provided them with such a son-in-law when they knew of other English servicemen who held to their faith and were being allowed to marry Maltese girls with the usual condition imposed by the Church that the offspring was to be brought up in the mother's faith. Not to mention the few who without having a husband, were giving birth to fatherless bastards.

Now happily married to a catholic George, Maria had no problems. Even the fact that because she was Maltese there were neither married quarters provided nor the alternative of an allowance. She was convinced things will change. After all Malta was now British for keeps.

A more worried man should have been Carmelo Borg. He had always been a ship chandler and made good money. He remembered the first years of the British in Malta when there were some 7000 ships entering Grand Harbour every year. All of them wanting water and victualling. With the outbreak of plague the number had heavily dwindled down to only a few. With the epidemic over there was still no respite since Malta was to remain in quarantine for a full 14 years. It was only the British effort to improve the situation that was making things move again, now that Malta had become a British colony. And 1815 had raised the number of ships coming into harbour to 3000. Not that this brought him enough earnings. But there was always that extra something to be made from contraband. He could also find the occasional British sailor too ready to part with some property in exchange for some Maltese delicacy or even money. And whether he got an English type of loaf, a flannel vest or a chunk of meat, Carmelo could always sell this at a profit.

The pre-occupation of Canon Francesco Saverio Caruana was of a different nature. He had led the Maltese rebellion against the French. With all the sacrifices entailed, and his being a clergyman. He had also worked hard to have Malta form part of the British Empire, and he did all this because he felt this was for the best of his country. On that point, there was no cause for remorse. And he was proved right when it became evident that the new rulers were respecting Maltese religious beliefs and helping to have them maintained. He had felt so proud when on 27th January, 1816, Pope Pius VII had conferred the preeminence and prerogatives of a Cathedral on the Church of St John of Valletta. He had had no say in the matter, but he was convinced there must have been a British element involved. Still, now that all he had worked for had materialised, he was expecting something in return. Indeed, he was a priest, and should have not entertained thoughts of compensation where a patriotic duty was concerned. But he was also a human being. There had been the temptation to hope, some years before, when on the initiative of Sir Alexander Ball, Monsignor Mattei was made the first Maltese Archbishop of Malta. But nothing of what he hoped for had materialised. Not even an archdeaconship. Perhaps it would be worth getting closer to Maitland as he had done with Ball.

Had he done so it would not have availed him anything. Not with Maitland. Particularly now, at a time when he had discovered a gross case of corruption in the *Università* which was the body holding the monopoly in importing grain and other foodstuffs. It was serious because of the consistent showing of a loss when the business should have shown a profit, and also by the fact that it was depriving many of small luxuries and also the essential things. This might as well have been a factor to make people grumble and revolt. Maitland got to the bottom of the embezzlement and found the main culprit. Yes, it was another Englishman. It seemed there had been a string of this type; Eton, Cochrane, and now Livingstone, who was a Head Jurat from the time of Ball and supposed to look over the Maltese Jurats. Maitland sacked him and took over the whole operation under government control until it could be properly organised and given back to private enterprise. He also had time to re-organise government departments, change the system of public accounts and property and reformed both hospitals and charitable institutions. How could a man do so much? He could because he was dedicated to the serious and had no mind for frailities.

How much this was so can be deduced from his sarcasm when his opinion was sought in connection with the institution of the Order of St Michael and St George originally proposed to reward the services of distinguished Ionians and Maltese. The original name suggested for the Order was that of Saint Spiridion.

"That would do well for the Ionian Isles," said Maitland, "but the saint is not in such high feather in Malta." So he suggested the poetic name of St John of the Isles. But finally it was decided to adopt those of St Michael and St George.

"The riband ought to be black and red," he told them, "showing more red than black, however," and continued to indulge in further banter when they showed him the sketch of St Michael encountering Satan. "That saint looks too tame to me," he said.

Indeed, letters patent constituting the Order were issued by George III on 27th April, 1818 and on 16th December of the same year, there was the investiture of the first five distinguished persons conferred with the Order. As Knights Grand Cross there were Rear Admiral Charles Penrose, the Naval Commander-in-Chief, Dr Giuseppe Borg Olivier, President of the High Court of Appeal and

Member of the Supreme Council of Justice, and Dr Raffaele Crispino Xerri, a Member of the Supreme Council of Justice. As Knight Commanders there were Judge Giuseppe Nicolo Zammit and Richard Plasket, the Chief Secretary to Government. The ceremony was held in the Throne Room of the Grandmasters' Palace in Valletta which thenceforth was to be called The Hall of St Michael and St George, as it is still called to-day. There was a Royal Salute fired by forts and ships in harbour, and in the evening a banquet was given by the Naval Commander-in-Chief (the new Knight Grand Cross) followed by a State Ball at the Palace.

There were by now so many reforms in the offing, all toed by the British Government, that they might have overshadowed the country's true plight. Maitland's achievements were useful but they were not producing the much wanted respite to the man in the street.

In an attempt to try and remedy the situation there were the leaders who tried to see what was happening in the working sector of the United Kingdom. Hoping, no doubt, to base what claims they could make, on what Britain was doing with her people. But even there the situation wasn't so rosy. The British labour sector was passing through the turmoils which had followed The Combination Act passed as far back as 1800 which had made it illegal for workmen to combine for the purpose of improving their conditions of labour. This oppressive legislation had sprung largely from the revolutionary ideas that were at the time radiating from France and was now causing much unrest. No one in his senses then could hope for something better to be done for small Malta, the latest British Colony.

So against this background Maitland's energy and unselfish dedication still lent courage. And the military pageantry that had now come to the island warmed the cockles of Maltese hearts. Notwithstanding the fact that it did not provide the much wanted bread for the majority of 100,000 inhabitants. It was then against all expectations when the merchants went up in arms against government's prolonged monopoly on the importation of corn which Maitland had introduced. This time they appealed to the House of Commons and to everyone's surprise it was abolished. This was of course only going to provide a long term relaxation on imports with a chance for the merchants to make that little more money. It was not going to provide the work or cheaper prices. But it was enough to throw the country in a dilemma as to whether there should or not be made other claims and complaints.

So while the people continued to ponder in two minds, Maitland carried on with his efforts. He never stopped trying. Whether this had to be done in Malta, in confrontation with the British Government or in Rome where he was often going now about Church matters. He was even trying to carry out an educational reform which had lagged behind, and as an interim measure tried to prevail on Maltese parents to have their children educated in England at government's expense. But in this he did not succeed because of the lack of response. Then on 17th January, 1824 while he was dictating despatches in the morning, Maitland was seized by an attack of apoplexy. A few hours later he was dead.

★　★　★

Malta was stunned by his demise. Even the elements that had at some time had tiffs with him knew that the country had lost a friend. General feelings were now torn between loyalty to Britain and hope she would make up with a good substitute, and distrust which bred fear of an unsuitable man.

However, His Majesty's Imperial Government was not in a position to ignore Malta. Not because of any singular feelings but because the situation in the Mediterranean dictated it. The Greek War of Independence which had broken out in 1821 was not getting any better and was beng marked by terrible atrocities. The Greeks, torn as they were by factional quarrels could not be expected to unite and present a common front to Turkey, and many powers that were sympathetic with the country to which Europe owed so much in the intellectual sphere felt that they could not let it be destroyed. There was also the question of their Levant trade which would be jeopardized were Greece to fall. All of these being factors to indicate that those powers might have to intervene should the situation worsen. And

Britain was one of them.

So to take Maitland's place there was chosen a man with a record of good service behind him. Francis Rawdon, Marquis of Hastigs had been Governor General of India, where he had excelled himself by establishing British power even at the expense of having had to go to war against military states. The news that preceded him described the new governor as an able and industrious administrator. The British blew his image further by adding that he was not only a peer but also belonged to the Irish nobility, and as the Earl of Moira he had sat in the Houses of Commons on both sides of the Irish Channel. It was only when he arrived in Malta in January 1824 that the people knew he was seventy and probably at the evening of his days. Still, they welcomed him and hoped for the best.

It is not known whether and how much Hastings had been briefed before his appointment, but it doesn't appear that he knew of the real situation. For he did not fail soon after his arrival to express his distress at the situation he found. The biggest contrast with the many good things he knew about Malta, he said, being the poverty amongst the majority, and the most popular occupation seemingly being that of the beggar.

Some historians tend to place Hastings as having been much inferior to Maitland. There are those who also say that only the embarrassment he had with his private affairs and his fortune being at a low ebb made him accept the governorship. It is not known how true was this, but it cannot be denied that he certainly did not possess the fiery zeal and aptitude of his predecessor. Yet the swift way in which he acted to improve the Maltese lot was a novelty following the time lagging, however useful reformations were in the offing in Maitland's time. It immediately occurred to Hastings as indeed had happened with his predecessor, that commerce had to be expanded if there were to be provided more work and earnings. But instead of looking for outlets, he preferred to tackle the difficulties, and there immediately emerged the strict quarantine regulations which were prohibiting shipping to call at Malta for 14 years from the outbreak of plague. So rather than waiting and hoping, he took energetic action to repeal these regulations and induce Mediterranean states to start allowing their ships to call at Malta again. Effect was immediate, and with the availability of shipping, Hastings now turned to rebuild the stagnant export of cotton grown in the island to the United Kingdom, where the British Government agreed to have it admitted free. With the fast expansion of the British Navy it occurred to Hastings as well that there could be a place for Maltese recruits in this service. And indeed his suggestions found ready ears in the Admiralty who ordered Officers Commanding His Majesty's Ships in the Mediterranean to take on Maltese recruits, but limiting the intake to the proportion of five men to every hundred British seamen. This arrangement was also extended to the military regiments. This was not all. There had to be some other arrangements to offer relief to the expanding population and Hastings struck on the idea of suggesting migration to some other country which lacked manpower for available work. There was Cephalonia which qualified. One of the Ionian Isles which belonged to Britain. Any critics of this scheme because of what was termed exile from one's country could not know this was a safety valve for Malta's characteristic expansion when work gets less and which was to be used more than a hundred years later.

For those who had a trade but no job, and did not want to leave their country, Hastings launched a scheme whereby these could be provided with food and lodging together with tools and apparata to exercise a trade for which they were not paid any emoluments. These being made up by the money spent on their subsistence. In this too he seemed to be setting the shape of things to come in the distant future.

Hastings was no reformist but he reviewed some of the reforms started by Maitland, and that in Education was one of them. His intervention was without much fuss and fireworks but had a big effect on Malta's posterity. He was lucky in this respect to find the assistance of John Hookham Frere who was a retired Under-Secretary of State in the British Foreign Office that had settled in Malta in 1820 owing to the state of health of his wife, the Countess of Erroll. When he was not indulging in his writing or learning Maltese and Hebrew, Hookham Frere was helping with his benevolence and philanthropic activities. So he gladly accepted Hasting's offer to chair a commission formed up to revise the course of studies in the University. And it was on his insistence that the study of Maltese was introduced in the curriculum.

It will be remembered that the Maltese language was until now a spoken but unwritten tongue, but fortunately enough there had been a Maltese scholar, Mikiel Anton Vassalli, who had reduced its vernacular to a grammatical system and became its first teacher. It was him and his grammar that were then introduced into the University to give birth to the language that is written, studied and spoken to-day.

This could be said to have given birth to the present Maltese language which will be always remembered as having occurred under British rule. Its meaning was not realised at the time and Malta carried on as before. There were little or no problems for the well to do. Their conditions had never changed. Whenever seamen or soldiers of the garrison behaved arrogantly as was becoming the habit, this made them more conscious of their status and they behaved accordingly to the Britishers' misdemeanour. It was different with the rest however. These had to submit if they did not want to court trouble. The housewives made their purchases when they found them or the money to pay, and cooked for their families when there was something to cook. When there wasn't any coal for the *kenur* or stone cooker they would have resort to firewood collected by husbands and children. When there wasn't any of this either, then the family would have to go on a cold diet whether they liked it or not, which would certainly have bread as its main and basic item, to go maybe with a soft cheese made from goats' milk, or have the bread soaked in oil and a tomato splashed over it.

All depended on the husbands who continued to provide, however meagre, when they worked. When they did not, then they would have to resort to something else. Like doing odd jobs for pennies; or getting their hands on some swill disposed of for a pittance by naval canteens. In the right season they could provide a delicacy in common snails. It was very easy for them to clamber over rocky hill-sides and gather them after heavy evening dews. Soaked in salt water and cooked they made a delicious meal and when seasoned with capers which were also easy to get. However, when all methods failed to provide there was always the wide human charity to resort to. Many friaries had daily queues of men and women at noon, waiting for their portion of the local minestrone which the monks always provided for those who cared to go and get it. The literate classes too who still led their life as bounded by convention and tradition were never lacking in their sense of responsibility to help the less fortunate. And although there were many who had fallen on hard times there had never been any death from hunger.

But now there was cause for reflection. The young men and women who had been born under British rule did not know of any other kind of life. But the elders could make comparisons with time under previous occupations. They could realise now that there had been no improvements in living conditions in the first 24 years of British occupation. There were those who stopped there and didn't grumble. For them their unfortunate situation was the will of God, and they neither blamed anyone nor made any comparisons with the British which they could see around them. For others, however, it was an anathema and a problem.

The British Government had a problem too in that it had failed to reach its original objective of turning Malta into the intended fortress. It was true that the Mediterranean fleet had been increased, and from one first rate ship and seven smaller ones in 1815, now had 3 first raters and 27 others. But nothing had been done in the way of improving harbours and fortifying the island. This point was driven in when the army of Mehmet Ali, the Pasha of Egypt landed in Morea to subjugate the Greeks who were still fighting the Turks. Britain had been morally bound to help the Greeks and this could mean war, with her base at Malta being within reach of the fighting. Now when it was already late there was sudden realisation that she had been overtaken by events, and of how much time had been spent in endeavours to create a new status for Malta and openings for work without any tangible results. There was then a belated impetus to do something. Perhaps Hastings could be consulted. He had produced some good ideas in the past. But now he was away with HMS *Revenge* which was somewhere near Naples. He could of course be called back. However, by the time someone thought of doing it on 28th November, 1826, Hastings was dead. There was only his corpse to be brought back and buried in the gardens that still bear his name.

If Hastings' death had spoiled what plans there were in the offing, it could in a different way have been a blessing in disguise offering possibilities to the British Government now aware more than ever before of some form of retrenchment that had to be made in anticipation of what plans were to be rushed for Malta. Whatever cuts had to be made in expenditure must not in any way effect the Maltese. It wasn't the right time for it. There was then the lowering of the post of Governor to that of Lieutenant Governor for whoever had to fill it. This would reduce on the salary and allowances. It was therefore as a Lieutenant Governor that Hastings' successor, Sir Frederick Cavendish Ponsonby was appointed in 1826. As for the other matter of Greece that was more pressing, the British Government turned to the other involved powers Russia and France, in an attempt to find a way out of the impasse without risking a war.

Ponsonby turned out to be a very simple man who had distinguished himself in the Spanish campaign and was seriously wounded at Waterloo. He was in fact deprived of the use of his right arm. He was endowed with a sweet temper and gentle manners. But although he had had a lot of experience he might not have been the right choice for those times. Maybe he knew this himself too. And that's why he took up Sir Frederick Hankey as his right hand man. Hankey was both strong and clever, and time was to show that many of Ponsonby's decisions were to be his. Had be not been there, it is wondered whether the British Government would have readily agreed to start pumping an annual contribution of £150,000 into Malta to help with the general difficult situation.

Another of Ponsonby's first acts, no doubt promoted by

Hankey, was to bring to the surface the increased rate of piracy in the Levant which was lessening trade in the Mediterranean and bringing poverty in Malta. It was very likely that this had existed before but had become more conspicuous by the Turkish and Egyptian successes in Greece. Which hastened Britain and her allies to act. The representatives of the three nations met in London and signed an undertaking to offer their mediation services to the conflict. But with the condition that Greece would be allowed free as a self-governing state. When this was transmitted to the warring nations, Turkey refused to consider it, however. So there was no way out. In preference to declaring total war Britain, Russia and France sent their combined fleets to attack the Turks at Navarino on 28th October, 1827. This was only the first step, carried out with the hope that Turkey would accept the offered terms. After the battle the allied fleets returned to Malta to await results.

Never before had the island's harbours witnessed so many warships. All beflagged and carrying the victorious look. For the days that followed Malta was on fete. But there were also the ships that had to undergo repairs and the dockyard began working round the clock and engaging more labour. The British and foreign seamen went ashore generating much business for boatmen, bars and shops. Artisans too had their hands full to supply what was required by the foreigners. Ship chandlers had to call on more farmers, butchers and other food suppliers to meet their orders. Suddenly there had dawned a time of plenty and a lot of money was changing hands.

Encouraged by this victory, the allies turned to stamp out piracy, and an Anglo-French squadron under Sir Thomas Staines was despatched to the pirates' lair in Carabusa in Candia and there destroyed every vessel found in harbour. The Eastern Mediterranean was swept clean of pirate ships and what pirates were captured were taken to Malta. Writing about the occasion, Admiral Codrington described the island's prisons as being packed with pirates. The French wanted to deal with them summarily while the Russians favoured killing them straightway without a trial. It was only the English Admiral who insisted on going by the law. Still, the Vice-Admiralty Court was kept very busy. And even the hangman had to work overtime.

Malta had never had it so good. What nobody knew was how long it would last. But whether it was to last long or not there was the message spelt loud and clear to all concerned – that the island's livelihood was closely tied up with the naval base and garrison.

While this part of history was being made, Britain was trying to contribute her own. It fell to Ponsonby to try and push forward with a reform which none of his predecessors had managed to do. This was because of its delicate nature and risks of hurting Maltese religious feelings since it involved temporal matters of the Church. It was a reform meant to suppress the law of sanctuary and also to abolish ecclesiastical exemption from lay jurisdiction and giving of evidence in courts of law. It was more of a British political gamble to be hidden behind the soft person of Ponsonby who soon transferred responsibility to Hankey and sent him to Rome. It wasn't that easy to persuade Pope Leo XII, but finally Hankey returned to Malta to issue the relevant proclamations on 10 April, 1828.

It was a victory for an enthusiastic Ponsonby who was soon reporting to the Secretary of State the absence of any reaction from the population. Indeed none had objected. Neither the people nor Monsignor Francesco Saverio Caruana who had since been elevated to the rank of Archdeacon, which took him closer to the bishopcy he had for so long desired and expected. It is more than obvious that Ponsonby and his masters in Britain were banking on Monsignor Caruana's well known attachment to the British Government and that this would make him do their bidding. But it was nothing of the sort. Monsignor Caruana's silence in front of the new reforms with which he might not have agreed was borne only from an inner conflict of knowing of the force that was being mounted on the Maltese side for another attempt to obtain political liberty. And his was only a diplomatic silence.

The new movement was started by a certain Camillo Sciberras, the son of a Maltese baron, and who had received his experience of fighting for political liberty from the French. He had worked for them during the occupation, and had even gone with them to France when they had left. Now he had returned to Malta and home imbued with new ideas which he was using for his country's needs. Helping him there was a George Mitrovich, who notwithstanding his Slav sounding surname was a Maltese. He was indeed very much pro-British, but was always criticising their administration in Malta. Between them two, Sciberras and Mitrovich formed a committee to enlist public support. This wasn't difficult. Russia had resumed the offensive against Turkey by marching on Constantinople, and the French moved to drive the Egyptians out of Morea. So their respective fleets had left Malta, and the squeeze in earnings began to be felt again. The people were restless, and they could not but listen to their leaders who had bided their time for their quiet assault on their ruler. A Britain weakened by her recent intervention in local religious matters and coming so soon after the Emancipation Act passed by the Wellington's Ministry in 1829 whereby Catholics had been admitted to both Houses of Parliament and to all offices, civil and military.

What might have been considered as a last way out of the political avalanche Ponsonby could foresee came with the death of Archbishop Mattei on 14th July, 1829. So Monsignor Caruana was immediately recommended for appointment in his stead, because of his ability, integrity and his firm attachment to the British government as well as his acceptability to his fellow-countrymen. But this had no effect on the now determined political leaders. And soon after, the appeal was made. Not for anything touching on the religious as Ponsonby might have expected, but for a free press, removal of the strict censorship and what was more important the granting of a legislative assembly to be elected by the free suffrage of the Maltese.

It was to take years before both these matters could be resolved. So Archdeacon Caruana had to wait in suspense as Hankey battled his case in Rome, while the Maltese under Camillo Sciberras and George Mitrovich had to steer their way through the obstacles that were raised. Even to the extent of Mitrovich having to go to London to enlist the sympathies of members of Parliament. One of these, William Ewart the member for Liverpool subsequently published a pamphlet – *The Claims of the Maltese founded upon the Principles of Justice.*

The appeal, a further example of Maltese sober rectitude which by now had impressed the British people, struck home. And the British Government expressed its willingness to grant a legislative assembly of about thirty Maltese to be elected by the free suffrage of the heads of families, proprietors, merchants and followers of the liberal professions of art. The only difficulty was now raised by Ponsonby because, he said, this would place the Governor between two stools – the wishes of the Assembly and those of the Secretary of State. But he had to withdraw this objection in the light of further reforms he had intended, and as a compromise he suggested a legislative council of nine which was accepted by the British Government. In the meantime, on 28th February, 1831 Monsignor Caruana received his appointment as Bishop of Malta. On 1st April, 1835, His Majesty William IV gave *Instructions* for the constitution of the Legislative Council.

Although constituted, unfortunately this council did not function immediately. There were too many elements, mostly British, who were interested in maintaining and perpetuating the existing feudal system. They raised so many difficulties on other reforms which they wanted to be incorporated that there was even felt the need for a Royal Commission. When things became too complicated the British Government was finally obliged to advise His Majesty to order a formal inquiry before the Council could be expected to function freely.

Ponsonby had in the meantime left Malta, obliged by his state of health which did not permit him to face the worries of the situation. When things got to a head, he resigned his Lieutenant Governship.

Nonetheless, even if it had to come after 35 years of occupation, this significant Maltese achievement is considered to have been the first step on the road to emancipation in their glorious history.

CHAPTER IV

REVELATIONS OF A VICTORIAN MALTA

It would here be worthwhile having a look at the other end of the scale and see what image was projecting on the British side. Until the beginning of the 19th century there was nothing of such an image to speak of and Malta must have been a nonentity to the general Briton. A few might have found the name mentioned in their history books to be associated with a far away island where the Knights of St John had established some sort of civilisation. Maybe also dismissing this with a shrug to put the Maltese into a popular category of a mixed race of Italian Arabic stock suffering from the misfortune of not being English. It was in 1802 after the signing of the Treaty of Amiens that the name of Malta spread wider in the United Kingdom. Drawing more popularity no doubt after both Houses of Parliament and the press criticized the Government for letting the island go to the Order of St John.

It must be said, however, that if Malta had been so far removed from British minds, the same could not be said of the Order. This had for so long represented in the minds of Europe the hope of a unity that it had become hard, even for Protestant statesmen, to abandon this concept. When, for example, the King of Bavaria had wished to revive the dormant Anglo-Bavarian Langue, offering to endow it with the expropriated lands of the suppressed Jesuits in 1782, the Order had formally sought the approval of the Protestant King George III of England. The monarch had vacillated, ostensibly awaiting the Pope's reaction, but finally in 1783, signified his approval, addressing the Order as from one Sovereign to another.

So after Britain had taken over Malta under her protection and the different governments were receiving and discussing both statements and petitions from the island's people, these failed to impress. There were those on the British side who were more loyal to the strictly Protestant Nelson tradition and had even established an Order oif Malta within Freemasonry. These could certainly not lend their support to a Malta which had drifted away from the Order. There was also the question of the predominant catholic religion which seemed not only to have a finger in every Maltese pie, but to rule every element of the islanders' life. This had from the very start become an anathema for protestant diehards. But the general parliamentarian soon ceased to think of Malta as just another British colony inhabited by natives who were exclusively engaged in the dockyard when they were not priests, monks or nuns. As it was being intimated. Still, many a despatch from respective governors was now calling for debate which more often than not had a divided house. Fortunately enough this situation did not seem to have reflected itself in the general Briton. There were already by now the first Maltese wives being taken home by their British husbands, to stay and mix with their counterparts. However, the little that was being learned about Malta was only through the few impressions brought by soldiers and sailors largely gleaned from bars and haunts of the least reputable in the island.

One of the first to shed some light to Britons was Samuel Taylor Coleridge who on his return to England from Malta had written poems in the form of a sustained panegyric to Sir Alexander Ball for whom he had had a great admiration. But he had also shown Ball's sympathy for the island.

To follow in Coleridge's steps four yers later there was George Gordon, the sixth Lord Byron with two sojourns in the island where he fell in love with Florence, the daughter, of Baron Herbert, at one time Austrian Internuncio in Costantinople and the wife of Charles Spencer Smith who was her father's colleague at the same Court. It was indeed this affair which had made Byron bring out some good points on Malta. In the same way as he had expressed distaste about the climate and ringing churchbells possibly because of the illness he was suffering from at the time, and made adverse comments on the stepped streets he had to climb because of his club foot.

By now, however, it was the age of the grand tour when young British noblemen and gentlemen of means descended upon France and Italy. It was the time too when there began to reach Great Britain romantic stories of a Malta full of English and Neopolitan nobility, and officers of the fleet and the garrison vying in their showy dresses with the foreign costumes intermixed with them. There were also stories being played to peculiar traditional festivals that the Maltese people, notwithstanding their adjustment to some British ways, were still holding, as they had originated and come down from the time of the Knights. Carnival was one of them which always had Valletta's narrow stepped medieval streets crammed with dancing, singing people of all shapes and ages. Groups in fancy dress which showed ingenuity and variety which would do the *Parata,* a dance to symbolize the Maltese victory over the Turks in the Great Siege of 1565. The defiles would follow, made up of floats with gigantic and lifelike papiermache figures of animals, birds and human beings. Where the floats did not reach there would be the pretty grls to dance and the stilt-men to march with great virtuosity. These festivities lasted for three days, all full of colour, gaiety and good humour. For the less adventurous there was bound to be some folklore festival like that of *Imnarja* (the name being derived from *Luminaria* because of the many illuminations by thousands of tallow or oil lamps). The festival was held on the 29th June, then being the national feast of St Peter and St Paul, with the main celebrations being centred at Buskett Gardens which were the island's only woodland. Dwarfed by the high imposing structure of the Castle of Verdala, used as the summer residence of British governors, and with acres of oranges, lemons and other fruit, as well as lofty pines, cyrpresses, oak and ash these gardens then offered, as they still do to-day, a welcome rest. But on the feast day there was spectacle with an agricultural show and fatstock competitions. In the evening there would be singing contests with men competing by chanting verses extemporised on the spot to the traditional lilt not unlike the Flamenco of Andalusia. The night then would be devoted to eating, with local rabit being cooked and served from open air stalls, and washed down with local rough wine.

A stream of visitors was soon going to Malta. Those who had business to mix with pleasure. Others out of simple curiosity to have a look at the place about which there was already so much talk.

It could be that none of the mentioned attractions had drawn the young Disraeli to Malta in August 1830. His visit there was only a prelude to his two year tour of the Near East, and he must have thought of Malta as an ideal venue for his most exotic and flamboyant affectations of dress and posture. He did a lot of sightseeing, and went places. Always dressed as a dandy and followed by a curious half of the population of the place. However, by time he forgot about his "buffooneries" as he himself called them, and the only recollections of Malta that remained with him and those who followed his example were of architectural beauties.

These goings and comings had become like a publicity campaign, always bringing something new and far out from what reached parliament, where the Protestant diehards kept nurturing their bogey and pressed for a subservient Malta to be kept in her place. More by mental rather than physical pressure which was often transmitting itself into an element of snobbery to be eventually reflected in the British that were in Malta. The representatives of this cult, because it had almost come to that, were by now already evidently keeping to themselves and not mixing with Maltese unless it was necessary. They had even opened their own clubs there, following the British Empire tradition, as if to put in a dilemma those who were trying to know and understand Malta. Elsewhere, they talked and used what influence they had to undermine. And where they did, theirs became like subversive voices.

But there was much more to tip the scales for a decision with the one person who could strike a genuine balance being Sir Walter Scott, who went to Malta on 21st November, 1831. Truly enough, Sir Walter went there in search of rest after his two strokes of paralysis, but he wrote enough of his three weeks stay to subdue what fires had been stoked by the British snobs. To what pictures might have been painted of the ignorant natives he wrote of the various courteous offers he received of houses where he could stay. What ideas might have been disseminated of Maltese backwardness were overshadowed by the stirring of his romantic soul to its very depths by the knightly glories of Valletta and the magnificence of St John's Cathedral enshrined with all the glorious wealth of colour and art that man could device. Even though Sir Walter had to spend time with members of the snobbery in Malta, and he had even to attend a ball given for him at their club, he never said a word about their line of thought. Instead, he had a lot to say on the older ambient of the island with its episodes of secular struggling against the Turks which made of her the last stronghold of chivalry.

It was symbolic of Scott's affection for Malta that his last work which he could not complete was the story of *The Siege of Malta*, and that it was to be the last of the Waverley Novels. In him the Maltese saw the image of the British people with whom they had decided to throw their lot and which they could see no more. If he had been such a good ambassador for the British people in Malta, he had also done the same services for Malta in Great Britain.

Malta was by this time riding the waves of popularity as a summer and health resort and being referred to as the "Fior del Mondo" (Flower of the World). And this was against the background of a Europe in turmoil. There was France torn by the July Revolution which sent Charles X into exile across the English Channel and brought Louis Philippe to the throne. The Belgians had ended their union with the Dutch, and the Poles rose against Czar Nicholas I. Revolutions had also broken out in Italy and Germany. Still, the British had to see more of their important people following the trail to Malta, now in bold contrast with their own turbulent situation of the 1830s, with its duels and gambling halls, sponging houses and Grub Street bullies. But in the meantime there were more political upheavals going on in Malta which they had to watch. And nothing would stop them now that they had become interested.

The last popular news they had had of the island was of the granting of a legislative council which was stopped from functioning by internal strife. This being generated by the same people who should have had primary interest in making it work. Then there had been the appointment of a Commission by the British Government whose terms of reference were to be to start from scratch and define once and for all the situation in Malta. This could bring out into the open what was good or bad, the genuine and subversive elements in the always boiling situation.

To work things out there was now in Malta Sir Henry Frederick Bouverie who had succeeded Ponsonby. And he had shown that he meant business when he got rid of Sir Frederick Hankey, the Chief Secretary and replaced him by one of his choice, Sir Hector Greig. But those who were following the situation were more impressed with the arrival in Malta of the printed Commission concurrently with the new Governor. Both elements looked like a tandem which spelt efficiency. There was a good omen when the commission was enthusiastically received by the Maltese themselves as if they sensed this would solve all their problems. The father of George Cornwall Lewis who was a member of this commission received the first letter from his son.

"We found ourselves floating down the full tide of popularity on our arrival," he wrote to him. "We made a sort of triumphal entry into the town. The streets were illuminated at night and we were amazed with all kinds of respect." Then he had sounded his first note of premonition when he continued to say: "This state of things, however, has not been of long endurance and we are already beginning to think of rotten eggs and dead cats."

This was an auspicious beginning, and interested followers in Britain ached for more. Bot notwithstanding the fact that the Commission worked fast, it could not publicize its findings until its first investigation was complete. So while British public opinion was kept curious and guessing, there was a story being made up in Malta. A pitiful story of poverty of farmers, fishermen, spinners and other labourers who had to work 13 hours a day to earn from 6 to 8 pence a day when employed, or something like £5 a year when working on their own. It was a story of suffering the likes of which had never been heard of. Not even during the bad old days of the Industrial Revolution in Britain. The few working at the dockyard and with the garrison earned their meagre wages, but there were many more who were unemployed and had to do something for dear life. When they weren't begging, they were stealing, and when they found themselves with their back to the wall they could only resort to emigration.

This had by then been extended to Egypt, Barbary, Costantinople, Spain, Sicily and even to distant Brazil, British Guiana and the West Indies.

It suddenly occurred to every one involved that Malta had never been in such a state. Not during any of the many periods of occupation by other foreign powers. And there had been a long list of them. Much less under the Knights. How was it that this situation had to materialize under the British? And after 37 years of occupation? It needed no wisdom to realise there had been something wrong. Not in the present situation which could not be denied, but in the many others differently described or overestimated by previous governors. However, the Commission's terms of reference were not to find faults but to remedy them. So it set down to its first job.

When the outcome of the first investigation became news in Britain there was commiseration and support. Eyes turned on the Commission. But before this could begin its work on 9th June, 1837 there was an outbreak of Cholera in Malta which spread like wildlife.

As if to make a sympathetic Britain a partner in sorrow, King William IV died at Windsor on 20th June, 1837. In true British tradition, however, the mourning soon turned into days of expectation for a successor; something which under other circumstances would have also affected Malta, with the people being so keen on coronation of English monarchs. But when Queen Victoria's accession to the throne was proclaimed on 17th July, the island was still gripped by the cholera epidemic. By the end of the month there were already 3,382 dead, and this out of a population of 123,000.

Life had to stay still until the epidemic was practically extinct in October with the dead reaching 4,253. But then things began moving again and the Commission began to act with much more impetus as if to make for lost ground. There was soon the news of changes being made in Charitable Institutions to take in more of the poor as an immediate relief to a by now deplorable situation. Tariffs were reformed to benefit commerce and indirectly increasing payment for workers. All salaries were adjusted while many sinecure offices were abolished to save money which could be used elsewhere.

There had now also come into the scene of action Sarah Austin. She was the attractive wife of the other member of the Commission John Austin and who had already made her mark in the field of education elsewhere. Being loathe to remain idle, she soon engaged herself on a very ambitious programme meant to achieve what previous governors had failed to do in education. She also found time and energy to lend to the manufacture of Maltese lace and other handicrafts and what was more important to place them in the British market. Even Queen Victoria herself who was following the steps of this brave woman was soon numbering herself as her client and there was a royal order for eight dozen pairs long and eight dozen pairs short mits, besides a scarf. And all this was being done over and above Sarah Austin's constant help to her husband and the commission with their educational reforms.

While all this was going on, Bouverie was by no means idle. He was trying to get to the bottom and find out the subversive voices that were behind the division of Anglo-Maltese relationship. Sarah Austin had already recognised the barrier that was being raised by a clique of old English residents who had been working to keep the Maltese *natives* at a distance from what they considered was British and from what they saw to be the only decent society. By wit and stratagem she was helping both her husband and Mr Lewis, the other member of the commission, to get round these people. But Bouverie was now more direct, and there was an instant shock in the United Kingdom when it was known that he had sacked Sir John Stoddard, the Chief Justice, who had been in Malta since the time of Alexander Ball. But now Bouverie showed him as having been one of the two greatest demagogues in the island. The other was Langslow, the Attorney General, whose life was one continual attempt to set himself up as a leader of a discontented factious party betraying at all times the most inveterate enmity to all persons in authority. It was a delicate decision that had to be taken and Bouverie proved himself to be the strong man to take it. With these two men out of the way certain reforms became much easier and Bouverie left no stone unturned to get them through.

It was then the time for the Commission to tackle the question of freedom of the press which strangely enough drew the first opposition from the Church for fear of what attacks could be made on the catholic religion. But again Bouverie was not being stopped for such a puerile reason, and he went ahead. And Britain agreed with him with such freedom being to the heart of every democratic nation. There had to be enacted a libel legislation first, and this was drafted for approval by the British Government. This might have provided an occasion for protestant diehards to stoke their still glowing embers into fires. But there was no reaction. If there were still any of such elements, as Bouverie believed there were, they had remained silent. And so did he. Knowing that only time and action would bring any such subversive elements into the open. Only that by this time the Commission had completed its work and had to return to the United Kingdom. Indeed, it left after more than an 18 month stay in the island during which it had provided more work, induced better pay and conditions, introduced more care for the poor, made possible the promotion of Maltese civil servants to the higher posts, introduced other reforms and initiated steps for the freedom of the press. When it had first arrived on the island there had not been a single elementary school in the villages. Now, when it left, through the efforts of Sarah Austin there were ten.

In the United Kingdom benign eyes were watching all this and it did not surprise anyone when Queen Adelaide, the widow of King William IV, on being obliged to seek a warmer climate after an attack of bronchitis, decided to go to Malta. The island was agog with excitement on being honoured with her visit, the first royal one since the 15th century.

On 30th November, 1838 even the weather seemed to compromise for the occasion, and the sun rose in a fiery splendour on a busy ant-like community. From the early hours of the morning, people were hurrying to find a place of vantage close to the harbour. It was no longer an empty harbour as it had been for many months, and the boats carrying seamen from ships to shore brought back the look that more than nostalgic had become essential for Malta's living. When the hour was close there was not a single empty space on the bastions and the jetties. There were then some moments of silence. Suddenly the crowds broke into continuous cheering as *HMS Hastings* swung in towards the harbour entrance, with the frail little figure of the flaxen-haired queen standing on the deck. Then the clamorous shouting was drowned by the saluting guns and the clanging of church bells.

In going round Malta during her stay, the Queen met and spoke to people and endeared herslf to everybody. English and Maltese, of the higher class who spoke to her in English, and of the lower who could only smile in reply to her greetings. There were also those who spoke to her about the lack of a place for Protestant worship, and the Queen promised to help. Indeed she wrote to her niece, Queen Victoria, suggesting that there should be a Protestant Church in Malta, but the British Government regretted they could not do it. This confirmed what had already emerged elsewhere that what troubles had arisen in this context were not of the British Government's doing. But to put oil on troubled waters, the Queen agreed to erect the church at her own expense at a cost of £10,000. A site was selected in Valletta where there had been an unattractive German Auberge which was being used partly as a mill and bakery to the fleet, and partly as the residence of Sir John Stoddart, the dismissed Chief Justice, and on 20th March, 1839, just 11 days before her departure from Malta, the Queen laid the foundation stone to the singing of psalms and the firing of a royal salute.

There must have been very unwelcome thoughts crossing Bouverie's mind during the ceremony. Truly enough no one had objected to the building of the church and there was no indication that there would eventually be any objections. But he knew there might be those who would make capital of the situation. He certainly had no objection himself to have a Protestant church in Malta. But he did not want any trouble. Yet he still had a premonition that there would be. And with the Commission which had given him so much strength now gone, he was alone to face what difficulties were to be raised.

As the law of libel had not yet been approved, he could not go ahead with the introduction of the freedom of the press. But when he was pressed he compromised to allay any irritation by authorizing the publication of the first two newspapers under censorship — the monthly *Spettatore Imparziale* (Impartial Spectator) and the weekly *Portafoglio Maltese* (Maltese Portfolio). Still he had a hunch that there would be trouble. From where he could not say. And the situation had suddenly become like a thriller for him.

It was in February 1839 that the approved law of libel was received, and Bouverie had it submitted immediately to the legislative council where it was passed practically unamended on 14th March. Still there was no evident opposition, and more suspense. Could he have been wrong?

No, he wasn't. Among the journals that started right away there was *The Harlequin or Anglo-Maltese Miscellany*. Its editor was none other than Sir John Richardson openly backed by Sir John Stoddart who launched a vile attack. Not on the Government or the Maltese. But on the Church, well knowing this was the weakest point and likely to create trouble. Bouverie realized he had been right, but on the other hand another culprit and a subversive voice had shown its head. Or rather, the wolf had shed off its sheep's clothing. It therefore fell to him as governor to act and show his worth. The writer was prosecuted and condemned according to the new law of libel to a fine of 100 dollars or imprisonment for six months. Richardson chose imprisonment, no doubt hoping to creat more chaos. But after one month in jail during which membes of the House of Lords vainly tried to get a reversal of sentence, he paid the remaining part of the fine and was set at liberty. He followed with several petitions for redress, and when these failed he apologized and expressed contrition for what he had done. Asking of course to have his sentence squashed and the blot which was to mark him for life removed. But by now both Bouverie and the British Government were in the limelight. And with them there was Britain's prestige of her system of governing which had given much of what was best to Malta and some of what was worse. All to be continuously undermined by some movement to which this matter might have belonged. So they stuck to their guns.

There was no arguing with the fact that this episode meant more than a simple loss of face to Richardson and the movement he represented. Which might have brought on more pressure on an apparently adamant British Government to change attitude. What could have been an attempt to equilibrate the situation was a British endeavour to have an English bishop in Malta. This came about at this time when the pro-British Bishop Francesco Saverio Caruana was in bad health, and the Holy See was thinking of appointing a Coadjutor. The British Government quickly reminded the Holy See that no such appointment could be made without British concurrence. But while this exchange of communications was going on, there were instructions being issued against Bouverie's advice to Lord Holland, Her Majesty's Minister in Florence to ascertain discreetly whether Rome would object to the appointment of an English bishop should such a vacancy occur in the See of Malta. However, the English Cardinal Acton threw all caution to the wind and taking the bull by the horns proposed such a coadjutor direct to Monsignor Caruana naming four English Catholic ecclesiastics from whom a selection might be made.

This let the cat out of the bag, and to remedy the embarassing situation the British Government immediately recommended a Maltese, Canon Rossignaud as coadjutor, no doubt after ascertaining themselves of his feelings towards them.

But the Holy See was not deluded, and taking more time than was required to process the matter they did not make any appointment during Bouverie's term.

Bouverie remained four more years in office, with his term being extended beyond normal time. Had it been for sixteen thousand Maltese petitioners it would been extended for a second time. But he left on 15th June, 1843. His leaving was soon to be regretted both in Malta and the United Kingdom where in the following year the spiritual force of the italian *Risorgimento* was being stirred up from London by Giuseppe Mazzini, to be echoed by the many refugees constantly flowing into Malta from Sicily and Italy seeking protection of the British flag. And their spirit of reaction being infectious they were soon imbuing a local element with their ideas and contributing to the local press vicious attacks on the government. There was only the *Times* which did not subdue to this hostility. It was a situation which would have challenged Bouverie, who had been instrumental in obtaining that freedom of the press being abused. But in his place there was now Sir Patrick Stuart who could not handle such a situation. Indeed, nor any other from the looks of it, since he was also getting into trouble because of the rigidity of his opinions. Whether it was his disapproval of Carnival being held on a Sunday which caused enough trouble to have a British regimental band mobbed, or a new complaint by Protestant residents against the long laid condition for mixed marriages of the Protestant party having to bind itself to have children brought up in the catholic faith. He was at a loss in both cases, being helped out of his impasse by Gladstone in the first case and Lord Stanley, the new Secretary of State in the second. He made his mark with two secretaries of state and two governments. Then when he asked for leave and was refused, he resigned and left Malta on 23rd July, 1847.

There isn't much to be gleaned from Stuart's time. Even

the construction of the first dry dock which was being carried out owed its origin to the plans made by Bouverie for the development of Grand Harbour and the dockyard. The dock was opened in 1848 just after Stuart had left. Interestingly enough the only vivid picture of Malta of his time, heckled as it was by the Italian revolutionary element, was left recorded for posterity by William Thackeray in his book *A Journey from Cornhill to Cairo* after having been infected by the travel bug of the times and dropped at Malta in 1844.

"The entrance to the harbour is one of the most stately and agreeable scenes ever admired by a sea-sick traveller," he wrote. "The small basin was busy with a hundred ships, from the huge guard-ship, which lies there, a city in itself; merchantmen loading and crews cheering, under all the flags of the word flaunting in the sunshine; a half score of busy black steamers perpetually coming and going, coaling and painting, and puffing and hissing in and out of harbour; slim men-of-war's barges shooting to and fro, with long shining oars flashing, like wings over the water. Hundreds of painted town boats, with high heads and white awnings – down to the little tubs in which some naked, tawny young beggars came paddling up to the steamer, entreating us to let them dive for half-pence.

Round this busy blue water rise rocks, blazing in sunshine, and covered with every imaginable device of fortification. To the right St Elmo, with flag and light-house, and opposite, the Military Hospital, looking like a palace. And all round, the houses of the city, for its size the handsomest and most stately in the world."

Then he continued with his description, obviously after he had time to visit the hinterland.

"The streets are thronged with a lively, comfortable looking population. The poor seem to inhabit handsome stone palaces, with balconies and projecting windows of heavy carved stone. The lights and shadows, the cries and stenches, the fruit-shops and fish-stalls, the dresses and chatter of all nations. The soldiers in scarlet, and women in black mantillas. The beggars, boatmen, barrels of pickled herrings and macaroni. The shovel-hatted priests and bearded capuchins; the tobacco, grapes, onions and sunshine; the signboards, bottled-porter stores. And the statues of saints and little chapels which jostle the stranger's eyes as he goes up the famous stairs from the Watergate, make a scene of such pleasant confusion and liveliness as I have never witnessed before. And the effect of the groups of the multitudinous actors in this busy, cheerful drama is heightened, as it were, by the decorations of the stage. The sky is delightfully brilliant; all the houses and ornaments are stately. Castles and palaces are rising all around. And the flag, towers and walls of Fort St Elmo look as fresh and magnificent as if they had been erected only yesterday.''

This was a different picture being painted of Malta from others which had been shown until then. Indeed it differs even from what is sometimes being dished out to-day. It was a picture of a country with its well to do and the poor, but nonetheless all thriving in their particular type of activity. Which was the pattern of a sensible and industrious people, in a world of others, including Britain, with patterns that seemed to have little better to offer. It was evident that Bouverie had turned over an important page in British/Maltese history.

The British Government seems to have thought so too. For no sooner had the controversial Stuart made way and gave the British Prime Minister reason to pause and reflect that consideration was given to a suggestion that was transmitted from the people of Malta about allocating the island's administration and the garrison's command to different hands. There was sense in the suggestion and it was also the opportune time to give it a try. So the choice went for Sir Richard More O'Ferrall who at the early age of 38 had already become Lord of the Treasury under the Melbourne Administration and two years later had assumed the Secretaryship of the Admiralty and of the Treasury in succession. He was an Irishman and as a Member of parliament for Kildare had gained much experience. But what had made him more suitable for the present post of Governor of Malta was that he was a civilian. Moreover, he was a Catholic.

The selection of a Catholic for this post was a departure from usual procedure and its application substantiates the belief in Britain's determination not to let Malta fall back in the challenging times that could be seen ahead. In the island there had been a continuous increase of the repercussions from the Italian revolution and the continuous ebb and flow of italian political refugees was reflecting more than ever before the vicissitudes of the contestants in the Italian struggle for freedom. This was the first problem that faced O'Ferrall when he arrived in Malta on 18th December, 1847, which also coincided with the appointment of Monsignor Publio M. Sant as Coadjutor to the ailing bishop of Malta. There were objections raised to his appointment by the British Government since they had kept pushing their man, Canon Rossignaud for the post. But after much debate the Holy See's decision had finally prevailed.

What O'Ferrall and the British Government could not know was that notwithstanding their behaviour, many of the refugees, through their sufferings in the interests of their country, their exile and destituion, were arousing lively interest in their cause and sympathy for themselves amongst many Maltese. So when O'Farrell felt he had to stop them, in the interests of Malta, he could not foresee the reaction that was to be raised against him. Neither did the British Government which acceded to the governor's request and enforced an old legislation of 1818 requiring that no foreigner should be allowed in Malta without sufficient security. Despite its magnitude with the Maltese population this matter was still being considered as a minor one in the United Kingdom, particularly when O'Ferrall's primarily intended reforms began to be known. And he had begun with the one which he considered, and in fact was, the most important — the much awaited granting of a partly elected legislative council. This was to consist of 18 members of whom 7 were to be elected from Malta and 1 from Gozo. The remaining 10 were to be ex-officio members of whom half were to be Maltese. The first elections were held in August 1849. As was to be expected there were three ecclesiastics amongst those elected, while the member for Gozo was Dr Adrian Dingli. He was a 32 year old lawyer who had been called to the bar in 1837, and was to make a name for himself and his country in the years to come. It must have been for the first time that the British Government was raising no difficulties to the many schemes and projects that O'Ferrall was proposing. When there was the Criminal Code to be amended they noticed the name of Dr Adrian Dingli who though young, was piloting the discussion in council admirably. Before they knew it there was O'Ferrall again with a plan to build a prison on the system of Pentonville. There was one occasion when they had to disagree in 1850, to an amendment to the Criminal Code whereby offences against the Roman Catholic religion were to be more heavily penalized and described this religion as dominant in Malta while others were tolerated or protected. This had stirred the Anglicans to reaction and in order to avoid having the same old difficulties again after they were almost forgotten the Secretary of State objected to this amendment and had it redrafted.

Until now O'Ferrall seemed to be unpurturbed. He continued with his projects as if his life depended on them. He planned a lunatic asylum, improved hospitals, charities and the education system. He even established an Exchange and a Chamber of Commerce, while roads were improved. Commerce was aided by increased storage facilities and developed trade relations with other countries as well as a reformed Custom House. Her Majesty's Government did not find any difficulty in accepting his recommendation to have the President of the newly formed Chamber of Commerce, Agostino Portelli, knighted much to the disgust of the Maltese nobility. It was therefore against all expectations when Queen Victoria received a voluminous protest for the governor's removal.

The British Government were stunned as much as O'Ferrall was. He had been their baby or a sort of experiment that had worked. They could never understand how his system of administration which had rendered so many good results could have been described as a system of intrigue, favouritism and misrepresentation of facts. It was being alleged that all he did was wrong, unconstitutional, capricious and tyrannical. There was also an allegation that he had treated members of the Council of Government badly. Perhaps an inkling of what was behind the protest could be gleaned from the fact that it was sent by a Maltese political club and their anti-Catholic friends in England and Italy, led by Dr Gio. Carlo Grech Delicata. The club was a secret one which called itself *Associazione Patriottica Maltese* and was composed of a loud group who had already shown themselves as sympathising with republican ideas brought over by foreign refugees, as long as these implied an anti-government and anti-catholic nature.

What might have inspired such drastic attitude this time was the substantive number of British servicemen that were at this time embracing the catholic faith. Indeed there seems to have been such a wave of conversions. The Maltese Church still venerates the name of a local cleric Ignatius Falzon, who is accredited with a good number of these conversions. People still flock to his grave in a Valletta church seeking that which carries the portent of the miraculous. And there have been enough indications to date to initiate the laborious steps for the canonization of the Venerable Ignatius Falzon as a saint of the catholic church. When this is done, he will be the first Maltese saint. Also the saint of the British occupation.

The protest against O'Ferrall was ignored, but the governor being a sensible man by nature was hurt. So much so that he decided to leave. A petition signed by thousands of Maltese from among the nobility, professions, business community and the clergy did not hold him. Before he left on 13th May, 1851, his only consolation was a memorial of thanks he was given by those who worked around him. But his case went further to bring into the open the existence of subversive elements in British hierarchy which fact was to reflect much stronger on British Maltese relations later.

Rear-Admiral Sir Alexander Ball   (National War Museum Association of Malta)

Throne Room at the Grandmasters' Palace as altered in 1824/26

(National Library of Malta)

Saluting Battery overlooking Grand Harbour   (National Library of Malta)

Laying the foundaiton stone of St. Paul's Anglican Church on 2nd March, 1839
(National Library of Malta)

Celebrations on the 10th anniversary of Queen Victoria's accession to the throne
(National Library of Malta)

The Royal Opera House completed in 1866 (National Library of Malta)

Opear House damaged by fire in 1873 (National Library of Malta)

Auberge de Castille utilized as British Army Headquarters

Inaugural trip of Malta Railway on 28th February, 1883

THE MALTA GOVERNMENT GAZETTE.

Supplement to N° 1471.]   SATURDAY, 16th FEBRUARY, 1839.   *[Price 3d.*

All Public Acts appearing in this Gazette, signed by the proper Authorities, are to be considered as Official and obeyed as such.
By Command,   H. Greig, *Chief Secretary to Government.*

GOVERNMENT NOTICE.

HIS EXCELLENCY THE GOVERNOR is pleased to notify, that it is his intention to propose, after three weeks from this date, to the Council of Government for enactment the Ordinance of which the annexed is a Draft.

La Valletta 16th February 1839,
By Command of His Excellency,
H. Greig,
Chief Secretary to Government.

(DRAFT.)

AN ORDINANCE *enacted by the* GOVERNOR OF MALTA, *with the advice and consent of the Council of Government thereof, for abolishing the Censorship, and for providing against abuses of the consequent Liberty of Publishing.*

CHAPTER I.

SECT. I.—WHEREAS printed writings, printed in these islands, are liable and subjected to the censorship immediately hereafter described; and other printed writings are liable to the same censorship, although in practice they are not subjected thereto: And whereas it is expedient that the aforesaid censorship should be abolished:—Now his Excellency the Governor, with the advice and consent of the Council of Government, hereby enacts as follows:

From the day of the promulgation of the present Ordinance, no printed writing shall be subjected or liable to the censorship which is now exercised in these islands by Her Majesty's government therein.

SECT. II.—Whereas the aforesaid censorship will be abolished by virtue of the enactment in the first section of the present chapter: And whereas a liberty of publishing printed writings (printed in or out of these islands) will result from the abolition of the aforesaid censorship: And whereas it is expedient that the provisions against abuses of the aforesaid liberty of publishing, which are contained in the second and following chapters, should be substituted for the aforesaid censorship, on the abolition thereof :— Now his Excellency the Governor, with the advice and consent of the Council of Government, hereby enacts as follows:

From the day of the promulgation of the present Ordinance, the provisions in the second and following chapters thereof, shall have in these islands the force of laws.

CHAPTER II.

SECT. I.—THE only publications and contributions to publications, which are within the purviews of the present Ordinance, are publications of printed writings, and contributions to similar publications; and the only abuses of the aforesaid liberty of publishing, which are within the same purposes, are such publications, of printed writings, and such contributions to similar publications, as are prohibited in the third chapter and are not exempted in the fourth.

SECT. II.—Any words printed in alphabetical or other characters, and with types or in any other manner, on one or more papers or other substances, shall be deemed, for the same purposes, a printed writing.

SECT. III.—Any delivery of a printed writing to one or more persons, or any offer to deliver it to one or more persons, shall be deemed, for the same purposes, a publication thereof.

NOTIFICAZIONE DI GOVERNO.

SUA ECCELLENZA IL GOVERNATORE si compiace di notificare essere sua intenzione di proporre, dopo il lasso di tre settimane da questa data, al Consiglio di Governo per essere sanzionata, l'Ordinanza della quale l'annesso è un Abbozzo.

La Valletta, 16 Febbrajo, 1839.
Per Comando di Sua Eccellenza,
H. Greig,
Principale Segretario di Governo.

(ABBOZZO.)

ORDINANZA *statuita dal* GOVERNATORE DI MALTA, *col parere e consenso del Consiglio di Governo della medesima, per abolire la Censura, e per provvedere contro gli abusi della conseguente Libertà di Pubblicare.*

CAPITOLO I.

SEZ. I.—SICCOME gli scritti stampati, impressi in queste isole, sono soggetti ed assoggettati alla censura immediatamente qui appresso descritta; e gli altri scritti stampati sono soggetti alla stessa censura, benchè in pratica non vi sieno assoggettati: E siccome è spediente che la suddetta censura sia abolita: Ora Sua Eccellenza il Governatore col parere e consenso del Consiglio di Governo, colla presente statuisce come segue :

Dal dì della promulgazione della presente Ordinanza, nessuno scritto stampato sarà assoggettato o soggetto alla censura che ora è esercitata in queste isole dal Governo di Sua Maestà nelle stesse.

SEZ. II.—Siccome la suddetta censura sarà abolita in virtù della sanzione contenuta nella prima sezione del presente capitolo : E siccome una libertà di pubblicare scritti stampati (impressi in queste isole o fuori di esse) risulterà dall'abolizione della suddetta censura : E siccome egli è spediente che i provvedimenti contro gli abusi della suddetta libertà di pubblicare, che si contengono nel secondo e seguenti capitoli, si sostituiscano invece della suddetta censura, seguita l'abolizione di questa : Ora Sua Eccellenza il Governatore, col parere e consenso del Consiglio di Governo, colla presente statuisce come segue :

Dal dì della promulgazione della presente Ordinanza, i provvedimenti contenuti nel secondo e seguenti capitoli di essa, avranno forza di legge in queste isole.

CAPITOLO II.

SEZ. I.—Le sole pubblicazioni, e contribuzione a pubblicazioni, che si comprendono fra gli oggetti della presente Ordinanza, sono le pubblicazioni di scritti stampati, e le contribuzioni a simili pubblicazioni ; ed i soli abusi della suddetta libertà di pubblicare, che si comprendono fra gli stessi oggetti, sono quelle tali pubblicazioni di scritti stampati, e quelle tali contribuzioni a simili pubblicazioni, che si proibiscono nel terzo capitolo, e non si eccettuano nel quarto.

SEZ. II.—Qualunque parole stampate in alfabetici od altri caratteri, e con tipi ed in qualunque altra maniera, su di una o più carte od altre sostanze, saranno considerate, per gli stessi oggetti, uno scritto stampato.

SEZ. III.—Qualunque consegna ad una o più persone di uno scritto stampato, o qualunque offerta di consegnarlo ad una o più persone, sarà considerata, per gli stessi oggetti, una pubblicazione dello stesso.

Granting of Freedom of the Press in 1889   (National Library of Malta)

The Royal Navy of the 18th Century in harbour (National Library of Malta)

Presentation of Colours to Royal Malta Regiment on 1st January, 1895
(National Library of Malta)

Exequies held near the statue of Queen Victoria at her demise in 1901

CHAPTER V

THE FORTRESS AND DECADES OF CHANGE

The Crimean War brought an overnight change to Malta. Forty years of peace had doubtlessly slacked down Britain's war machine. But nonetheless commitments had to be honoured. In the days that followed the declaration of war there began to arrive British and French warships in Malta. As well as transports with thousands of troops. The harbours were soon packed with shipping, while Valletta and the outlying towns were swarming with servicemen, none of whom had ever fought. They were all looking at war with their youthful eyes seeing it more like a glorious adventure, and they made merry with all that Malta could give them, which brought brisk business.

The ships with the accoutrements of war that began flowing in generated work for everybody. And more money was soon pouring in. A boom had come to Malta, and it is still mentioned how smokers took the habit of plugging their pipes with gold sovereigns in those days. Maltese hearts had good reasons to leap with joy in the days that followed.

But hearts did not leap when the sick and the wounded began to arrive from the battlefield. With them they carried stories of scandalous treatment in the hospitals of Crimea which were soon to evoke the reaction of Florence Nightingale. The state in which those soldiers reached Malta, weakened by illness or crippled by wounds, touched hearts and consciences. The pitiful situation continued for months. But then, with their not being involved in it the Maltese were soon back to appreciate the monetary side of things, and it wasn't very long when they began slipping back into the easy going day to day existence.

It wasn't the same for the British Government. None could possibly miss the part Malta was playing in that war even though the theatre of operations was many hundreds of miles away. The island had become not only a port of call for all warships and transports proceeding to the Crimea, but had also to receive them back again with the wounded and to replenish stores. What repairs had to be made were carried out in the island's dockyard. All these being points to make one realize Malta's importance in any Mediterranean conflict. It was therefore more than obvious that the thought would occur as to what would happen if the island were to be some day attacked. And this brought home the fact that notwithstanding British original intentions of ruling a Malta that was a stronghold, no serious thoughts had as yet been spared to turn it into one.

It was true that the army had examined the extensive fortifications left by the Knights with some awe but whatever outcome there had been was dilatory and half-hearted. General Sir Patrick Stuart, a previous governor, had indicated his preoccupation when it was known that since 1845 the Mediterranean was swarming with the newly developed steamers of all nations. Except Britain who had stubbornly lagged behind.

"Before we might know of war," Stuart had said, "or could have any reinforcements from England, a few large steamers from Toulon, Marseilles and Algiers filled with troops, might in three or four days be off this island to attack us on both sides at once." The governor that had taken over, Sir William Reid too, who could better assess a situation now being mirrored by what was happening in Crimea, added his comments. "The English nation had been long accustomed to regard Gibraltar and Malta as impregnable fortresses," he wrote, "but a fortress is strong, only relatively to the means of attack brought against it. And the invention of steam navigation together with the formidable armament given to ships of war has changed this situation." These comments must have found fertile ground and generated the expected reaction for there were soon flowing into Malta, guns from the arsenals of England. New 10 inch guns and howitzers to replace the old 24 pounders which fired round shot through their smooth bores.

Maybe it was this sudden impetus which had made Reid agree with the proposed enactment of legislation by the Council of Government to have conscription for services in a Militia force for the defence of the island. However, this met with popular objections. The last time that Malta's able-bodied manpower was called up had been in 1792 when levies were called upon to maintain the siege of Valletta where the French had taken refuge. That had been a time of need, the people argued, but there wasn't any such need now to revert to the same situation. Particularly with the Crimean war now rolling towards its end, and Malta still riding the waves of plenty. But the people themselves wanted to give the council and government the benefit of the doubt as if to emphasize their good intentions. And the matter was referred in the form of a petition to Her Majesty's Government in London who found for them.

Because he was a militarily minded governor, it was considered strange when Reid became very much involved in Britain's long standing question of the Maltese bishopcy. It began with the governor's admiration of Canon Rossignaud, Britain's previous nominee who was still in line when Archbishop Sant became too old and ill for his office. Reid did not hesitate to revive Rossignaud's claim, and egged on by him, he called on the aid of Mr Lyons, the British representative in Rome. It was considered stranger still when the British Government did not press the claim. So it did not come as a surprise when after the Holy See presented its already chosen man – an Augustinian friar, Father Gaetano Pace Forno, there was a straight acceptance. The surprise came at the end when the British Government renounced to their always existing claim for right of nomination. All that was insisted upon now was the right to veto appointments in future. And that was how it remained after then.

Reid had also to endure another uncomfortable confrontation with the British Government at about the same time. It concerned the Director of Public Works, a Mr Arrowsmith whom he relieved of his duties following misappropriation of funds and a scandal involving a governess which had landed Arrowsmith in a matrimonial squabble. The British Government seems to have taken the view that Reid might have acted as he did because of his dislike for the man. Again it was a case to be straightened out by Dr Adrian Dingli. But Reid was eventually proved right when Arrowsmith was not found to answer the complaints made against him. He had run away to Costantinople. This wasn't a sporadic case of mismanagement by a British official. There must have been a few of them still carrying on the sequence of other unscrupulous British civil servants we have already met in previous times. The Victorian age seemed to have been rife with them. Another one to be ignominiously discovered was Fred Pedley, a Commissioner of Police who could hardly speak because of an impediment of speech. When Reid learned that he had reached his exalted posiion through the influence of his real father who had been no other than Sir Frederick Hankey, one time Chief Secretary and strong man of governor Ponsonby.

It was then Reid's turn to put his foot down to Lieutenant General Pennefather, the Army Commander in Malta, who had his own contribution to make to the rush for hastening defence preparations. His idea was to demolish part of Valletta to make space for a military hospital and bomb proof buildings.

"Oh no," said Reid in his comments to the Secretary of State on the matter contained in a despatch on 1st January, 1856, "the views and wishes of the Maltese will have to be considered in such a thing, as the sovereign state is of greater value than the shape of a rampart."

It is not known whether it was this stand that made the military authorities become |ticklish and abrasive. Reid wanted to go on with his plans and having already expressed himself in favour of expanding Grand Harbour's accommodation he proposed to have a canal cut to link this Harbour with the adjoining port of Marsamxett. He also availed himself of the opportunity of asking the advice of Robert Stephenson who happened to be in Malta on his way home from Egypt where he had been tendering advice on the building of a railway from the Mediterranean to the Red Sea. But when plans were concluded there was opposition from the army on the pretext that a canal would weaken defences. A state of feud and pique had developed between the army and the administration. And the politician was caught in the crossfire.

This state of affairs continued right into the term of the governor that followed, Sir John Gaspard le Marchant who took up the fight right away. It was now the turn of the British Government to sort things out. Letters were continuously pouring into the Colonial and War Offices from the respective contestants, and this at a time when Britain had already enough on her plate with the development of the big colonies like Australia and New Zealand which required more initial help than Malta. And there was also The Great Indian Mutiny which had to be stamped out. Nonetheless the best way out of the impasse was taken by having Pennefather transferred from Malta to Aldershot in 1859 and Le Marchant was given the command of the armed forces as well. One of his first tasks in the new role was to recommend that the Royal Malta Fencible Regiment, be converted into a better paid Artillery Corps. As for defence there was appointed a Colonel J.H. Lefroy of the Royal Artillery and Lt. Colonel H.C. Owen of the Royal Engineers and to them there was assigned the task of investigating and reporting on the situation.

In a way Le Marchant had also inherited a different Malta. With a population that was a new generation that had been born or brought up under British rule. It was a Malta that could see and feel the change it had gone through. Not in religion or national characteristics. Those had been left unchanged. But in life, customs and other attitudes learned from the British. There was also the change in that the new generations had bred more intellectuals. And these were no longer just priests and monks, but doctors, lawyers, engineers and others belonging to the professions. If the majority of the islanders was now feeling the pinch again, it was because of the blanks that were created after the end of the Crimean war. Blanks in trade, shipping and other activities that normally generated employment. And to this was added the increase in the cost of living, there were those who could analyse the situation reasonably. These were the people who remembered the beginning of their time in 1800 with something like 40 per cent of a population of 100,000 residing and making a living in the areas around the harbours. This had dwindled until 1840 to begin being boosted up by British defence spending reaching its climax during the Crimean war. Now that this had ended there was a slump. But this was in the normal trend of events, and could not be blamed on any-one. If the British had in their time learned that Malta could only thrive on defence, it goes to their credit that they had always increased their defence expenditure with the times. Indeed while this spending in 1840 had been only about £200,000 a year, in 1854 it had reached well over £400,000 and in 1856 exceeded £800,000. Now Le Marchant was increasing it again and making proposals for the construction of another port at Marsa in the inner part of Grand Harbour which would be deep enough for all kinds of vessels. He wanted to buy more land surrounding the creeks and enlarge the dockyard, which was also to be endowed with another dock. This might have all been done as a part of the drive for strengthening the naval base. But it could have also been in anticipation of the construction of the Suez Canal which was then being hotly discussed. It was expected that if plans for the canal were to materialize it would benefit Malta and her economy because of the greater number of ships that would have to use her harbours with the resulting trade. Truly enough British opinion was divided on the use of such a project. Disraeli had described it as a futile attempt, and Palmerston had backed him up. But Gladstone and the Lords of the Admiralty were all out for it. And so were the Maltese.

Colonel Lefroy's report had in the meantime been published and studied. It dealt mainly with weak points in the existing defences where an invader might penetrate. As an immediate outcome there were more guns placed in batteries installed at strategic points in Grand Harbour, Floriana, Fort Manoel, Fort Ricasoli and the Cottonera

Lines. There was, however, some amount of preoccupation and doubt since it was understood that if the strength and power of those defending guns had improved, so had the range increased of ships that might have to attack them. It was now 1861 and the Royal Navy had at last changed from sail to steam as a power for driving ships. *HMS Warrior* had been launched, steam powered and also plated with armour. Soon after there was the *Royal Sovereign* similarily arrayed, and mounting also four turrets, each of two 9 ton guns.

In the same way that he had reassured his authority over the military authorities when these wanted to intrude in civil affairs, Le Marchant did not miss the evolvement that was taking place in the population. It was now too that his recommendation for the Royal Malta Fencible Regiment had been approved by the War Office. So on 25th January, 1861 this regiment was converted into an Artillery Corps of six batteries with its officers being given the same pay as officers of the line with also an increase for other ranks. What might have irritated him was the behaviour of four members of the Government Council who were often harassing proceedings in a way that the 1849 constitution soon ceased to function as intended. This had indeed made him more autocratic, but he must be given the credit of having also looked at the other side of the coin and seen this attitude as emerging from the new emancipating nation. And no matter how much he might have been annoyed he still found the time and money, as well as the British Government's blessing for the improvement of roads and drainage systems as well as the building of dwellings at Floriana to induce the poor of Valletta to leave their slums. He also began the construction in Valletta of a new market on the model of *Les Halles Centrale* of Paris as befitting their civilization. To acknowledge their culture he built an Opera House designed by E.M. Barry the same architect who did Covent Garden of London.

The Crimean War, however, must have been an eye opener to many others, and in more ways than one. The way the harbour batteries at Sebastapol had mauled the Anglo French fleet might have had something to do with it. Because throughout Europe there had began a rush to strengthen power of coastal forts to outfight ships. The race was on. Never in the history of mankind had nations moved so fast. Speed became contagious, and the drive was soon taking on the proportions of a great contest.

It was expected that Britain would heed the indications. Particularly with their coming so timely when efforts were being made to renew the defensive capabilities of Malta. Lefroy's report in 1859 had started the War office on a race against time. Also against changes necessitated by new inventions to affect the conduct of war which began to appear with ever increasing rapidity. It wasn't just a question of altering buildings to increase accommodation for men and armour. Or to stregthen defence by additional buttressing. But also to constantly change guns even before any of them had as yet been fired in anger.

Even the remains of Sir Ralph Abercromby were affected by the hectic change, when they had to be removed from the salient of the bastion called by his name. To be taken to a new burial chamber of 1871 to make way for the construction of two casemates for two 10 inch guns to supplement the 9 inch ones placed in an adjoining site in 1867. The three Grand Harbour vanguards of St Elmo, Ricasoli and St Angelo were all involved in the changeover. As well as other bastions, curtains and cavaliers in the same area. The works costing £75,000. However, this was only a first stage in the renewal of the fortress. To herald a second one which was expected to cost much more in time and money. And also to quadruple the defences of Malta.

It was now time to put aside Lefroy's report which had contained mostly recommendations on inland defence systems. Instead, the services of William Francis Drummond Jervois were enlisted. He was a genius in the subject of forts and had only just been appointed Assistant Inspector General of fortifications. It was indeed his report in 1866 that paved the way for the further fortification of Malta. His plan took account of what had originally existed. Also to what alterations had been made. Not just in Grand Harbour area, but also elsewhere. As in the case of Forts St Lucian and St Thomas, two already existing vanguards which however had been supplemented by a hoop of guns firing out to sea through embrasures, apart from the renovated bastions to provide enfilade fire across the front of an enemy attempt to approach on land. But all this was far detached from what Jervois had in mind. His plan was for a new kind of fort to go with the times and he produced his design for the first one laid down in the form of an open fan in 1872. This was executed and completed in 1877 as Sliema Point Battery.

British engineers in Malta were soon working without a stop on the plans produced by Jervois, going in for a system of pairing, with forts always being matched more or less equidistant on each side of Grand Harbour. So with Sliema Point Battery on one side there was soon Fort St Rocco on the other. This system continued with St George's (later Fort Pembroke) pairing with Fort St Leonard, Spinola with Delle Grazie, and Fort Cambridge with Fort Rinella. The sequence was broken with three further forts intended to defend the eastern side of the island from Delimara and Tas-Silġ and the point called St Paul's Battery. This was a beautiful array of coastal forts, all capable of answering almost gun for gun, the firing from enemy men-of-war. But there was also allowance made for possible enemy landings and penetration. And a note of warning was sounded by the Inspector General of Forts, General J.J.A. Simmons, who went to Malta to see for himself in 1877. "The difficulty in maintaining a fleet in the Mediterranean without the possession of Malta would be almost unsurmountable," he said, "and if it were to be in the other hands, it would be a most dangerous point, from which the commercial route to Suez and the Levant could be obstructed."

There was then the additional determination to have no expense spared in fortifying the interior as well. This time the accent was on a system of fortifications on the high ground towards the western end of the island which would bring most of the inhabitants and all of their water supplies within the perimeter should an enemy force ever effect a landing. Four forts were to be built — Binġemma, Tarġa Battery, Fort Mosta and Maddalena. They would be made to tie up and stiffen a line of fortifications along the high escarpement running from coast to coast which was to be called the Victoria Lines. It was indeed a fitting name. Not as much because of their completion in 1897, the year of Queen Victoria's jubilee, as to their originality, so syntomatic of an age which produced the individual flamboyance of Victorian architecture.

To man the new fortifications the strength of the garrison had to be doubled to 12,000 men, absorbing also in the process the Artillery Corps which had once been the Royal Malta Fencible Regiment. The void here was soon to be filled by a new local infantry regiment — The Royal Malta Regiment of Militia which came into being on 1st May, 1889.

Between 1877 and 1887 it was estimated that Britain had spent something like four million pounds on these new defences. £2,314,757 on forts and works and £1,688,931 on guns. But there was also her navy which was at the time being converted and expanded. In 1897, the Mediterranean fleet based on Malta had grown to ten battleships, nine cruisers, seven gun-boats and fifteen destroyers.

At the time when the building of the fortress was taken in earnest to change the face of Malta, there was a different kind of development which was being overlooked. This concerned the people, with their economy, politics and other aspirations. Hitherto, British Governments of whichever party, had taken little interest in colonial matters and this is amply reflected in British attitude during this period of important change of Malta.

Following Lefroy's report on defence in 1859 there continued to flow into the island many Italian refugees of the Risorgimento. With all the increasing influence they were having on the population. Even if this was only through recounting tales of Bourbon profligacy. Fires that were started were soon being fanned by an ultra liberal party which became active with pro-Italian propaganda. And there was only a Britain to acquiesce because of her sympathy with the Italian movement. When on 14th March, 1861 she formally recognised the new Italian state which was already encroaching on Papal territory in preparation to its total seizure, there was a clash with Maltese ecclesiastical authorities who obviously sided with their pope.

Even though there were no British attempts to cover the

pill the tense situation was expected to calm down when the Italian exiles began to return home after Victor Emanuel was declared king of Italy. Only that those who left in the exodus were soon being replaced by adherents of the former regime. And now these lost no time to play on Maltese religious sentiments and stir animosity through the clergy and the press against the new Italian government which had Britain's support. This attitude persisted, and when Garibaldi called at Malta on his way to England on 24th March, 1864, there was still an element of hostility shown to him. Even if this was by a few, and very likely being inspired by a Bourbon element.

Nonetheless, to be pro-italian soon became synonymous with being anti-British. Finding also a badly needed idealogy in the deteriorating economic conditions, and making a scapegoat of a Britain only intent on building the fortress. Subversive elements soon found unexpected support in the untimely move of the P & O Company which for some reason gave up Malta for Messina in Sicily as a port of call with the resulting loss of commerce. And the situation would have deteriorated further had it not been nibbed in the bud by the timely opening of the Suez Canal in 1869. This changed both the strategic and the commercial situation of the Mediterranean, and Malta soon turned out to be the most convenient port of call for commercial shipping on the way from and to the East, and the new dominion of Australia. Overnight the island became an international coaling station, with an improvement in the economic situation. All antagonistic elements were silenced. Now the only discordant note was coming from the selfish British element who for no sensible reason whatsoever maintained an attitude of aloofness to the Maltese. This wasn't the inocuous behaviour of a few officers as some made it to have been. General Simmons, the plenipotentiary of the new government on defence had occasion to notice it later and to comment about it in 1877. He did not mince words to attribute to this selfish attitude what anti-British feelings were being generated and which would well undermine the foundations of the impregnable fortress his government was trying to build.

There is no doubt that this attitude, stringent enough as to debar even British junior officers from membership of the classy Union Club which was the nest and headquarters of the clique (some say it was done to prevent 'poodle-faking' with the seniors' wives) must have aided the division amongst the Maltese that emerged in 1870. With on one side an anti-reform group to present a picture of a feudal Latin upper class who would talk and write Italian, and drawing sympathy of most of the Clergy, the professional classes and Italianate landowning families. And the rest, being reform minded and remaining pro-British, speaking their Maltese language now a patois of Italian and Arabic with an admixture of Teutonic words and constructions, as well as their pidgin English. The former identified themselves with a still politically unstable and over-populated Italy, and found leadership in a lawyer, Dr Fortunato Mizzi. The latter were British minded more than the British themselves, and had Sigismondo Savona as their leader. Since the impetus of both groups was primarily emotional and sentimental, purely socio-logical or economic factors tended to draw collaboration from both. However, more than the ever present language question this division developed and brought into the open the two irreconcileable extremes of future Maltese politics.

More than this, then, it brought the big change. In the administration since by now the absolute majority of the heads of the various departments was made up of Maltese. Admittedly, drawn as were British Colonial officials, from a limited socio-economic group, but nonetheless having greater interest upon policy than is generally realized. Also in the people who were now carry-ing massive weight in the running of Malta's affairs. And as Britain was languishing in appreciation of her Disraeli for the mark he was making in his country, Malta too could count many of her sons who were similarily making her future. This was exemplified by Dr Adrian Dingli, whose abilities made him Attorney General in the time of Sir William Reid. Since then he had been knighted, and was now still the hub of the wheel of this big change. His advice had been continually sought by both British and Maltese authorities from the time of Sir William Reid, through those of Sir Henry Storkes and Sir Patrick Grant right to the governor of the day, Sir Charles Thomas Van Straubenzee. This had him very often called as the unofficial governor of Malta during his time.

Workers too, particularly at the dockyard, were following with awe the upheavals that were occurring in the field of industrial relations in Britain. There had been the Trade Union Act in 1871 which laid down terms under which trade unions could operate, and there was also the Employer's Liability Act of 1880 relating to those injured at work through the employers' negligence. From confusion in finding one's way there began to be realization that economic security was a widespread threat and beyond control of the individual. In 1884 the fitters at the dockyard tried to emulate British workers and form a trade union. They wanted to call it the Fitters' Union, with the only scope of creating its own funds to help members in illness or injury. But it was killed before it was born. Not by any British interference, but by Maltese who dubbed it as being a protestant organization, since it was being built on British rules. Any organisation with a British connection was in those days looked at with disapproval from the religious point of view. So the Fitters' Union had to change its structure to one of a Benefit Society, and its name to St Joseph Catholic Workers' Society. Also, this was to be in Italian. Any semblance to a trade union, had to be shed away.

This was an attitude now also to be reflected in the members of the council of government where besides the differing political interests there was appearing more surety of purpose in what was considered to be in the interest of the nation. Incredibly all could see and feel a change that had come. It wasn't a change in living and working conditions. There were still beggars in the streets and the rurals who by preference or compulsion still went about barefooted. As well as the urban Maltese of any special pretension who would wear a suit with the stiff collar, cravat and tie-pin. And the morning coat and top-hat for ceremonial occasions. But a change more intrinsic and characteristic in Maltese atitude itself. In the same way as their forefathers had strived for their rights with previous rulers so now those responsible were holding fast and speaking their mind to the British about what they considered right. No matter how much pressure was made by the War Office and the Admiralty on the Council to vote their share of £40,000 for an extension to a drainage system, the council stood firm when it was required to increase taxes to raise the money. In the same way that the British Government began sending experts like Rowsell, Sir Penrose Julyan and Keenan, so there was the local response. Giving way where it was due, but resisting where it was not. There was the feeling that an old flag had been hauled down, and never again would it be raised. That had faded. Instead, there was the image of a new life which was on a straight road where the crooked path had been. Even if there was still more suffering incurred to keep with it. Nonetheless there was the ordinary man in the street for whom this was something to be listened to without being understood. And he was more interested in building new and bigger churches, and to increase in fireworks for his village festa.

This was the general attitude being taken with the British Government. It was also the one being adopted between Maltese of different political belief. Dr Fortunato Mizzi and Sigismondo Savona often walked together to council meetings. But in session they pilloried each other. And when principles they held sacred were downtrodden they both resigned their seat which eventually led to the dissolation of the council. It had to be Sir J.D. Astley, the Parliamentary Under-Secretary of State himself to go to Malta and coax Dr Mizzi to return to the council, and assuring him in the process that Britain did not intend substituting the English language for Italian. Since this was the point that had made him resign. And when the old tune was played that the italian language question was only a cover for anti-British feeling, the anti-reformist party turned the tables down on its accusers by holding a well organised demonstration by a crowd of 30,00 to march into Valletta playing *God Save the Queen* and cheering the Governor, Sir Arthur Borton, who lost no time in confirming the loyalty of the Maltese to the crown notwithstanding what a picture of aggressiveness might have been painted of their new attitude.

The change had come about at the right time too. When Disraeli, now Earl of Beaconsfield, duly concerned for India was trying to check Russian ambitions in the Balkans. When the Balkan people were goaded into revolt which was repressed with barbarous cruelty by Turkish troops, Disraeli refused to join Russia, Austria and Germany in a protest. Intending, of course, to uphold the fading strength of Turkey to prevent Russia from increasing her influence in the Near East. So when the Czar decided to interfere singlehanded, Disraeli jumped a step ahead. The British fleet from Malta was despatched to protect Costantinople, and the island was immediately made to receive an army of 7,000 Indian troops to be sprung into action. Notwithstanding a better placed Aden acquired in 1839 which could be used as a base to control an Eastern situation.

Those times had introduced more than systems and philosophies into what had always been the Maltese way in dealing with Britain. And nothing had in any way spoiled the island's image. On 15th October, 1876 which was at the time of this activity, Prince Alfred, Duke of Edinburgh, who was Queen Victoria's second son, chose Malta as the venue for his wife, the Grand Duchess Marie Alexandrova, where she could give birth to a baby. When a daughter was born on 25 November, she was called Victoria Melita. Victoria after the Queen, and Melita as a token of respect for Malta. There was Albert Edward, the Prince oif Wales, to visit the island later that same year, and to be similarily welcomed with flowers and feasting which lasted three days.

In 1880 Disraeli had to bow out to Gladstone as the Liberals were returned to power. They already carried the tag of not caring for their empire. For them imperialism had always been considered as a hobby of a few enthusiasts. Any Maltese hopes, by now fervent, for an improvement in the island's constitutional status received a setback. But there was still occasion for Malta to be again in the limelight when following a mutiny in the Egyptian army which developed into a massacre of foreigners, Gladstone had to intervene to prevent Egypt from falling prey to anarchy with the risk of blocking the Suez Canal. The Mediterranean fleet left Malta to destroy the forts at Alexandria, while an army under Sir Garnet Wolseley, who had for a time taken Sir Adrian Dingli as his Chief Secretary in Cyprus, crushed the mutineers. Both operations, as always, had Malta as their springboard and base. But for the first time there was included with the attacking forces a Maltese officered contingent from the Royal Malta Fencible Artillery.

With such dramatic activity, and coming as it fortuitously did at a time when the whole world was astir, it would not be surprising if this period of Anglo Maltese courtship might have gone down in more than one book of history. All the major characters in the drama were well known, and whether they were quarrelling or coordinating efforts they must have been noted by all who had access to newsprint. Paramount in importance, however, was the return of the Conservatives to power in 1886, this time with Lord Salisbury as Prime Minister. Two years before, as fate would have it, Malta had a new governor. None other than Sir J.A. Lintorn Simmons who as Inspector General of Fortifications had been in the island in 1877 in connection with the new fortification on behalf of the same Conservative government under Disraeli.

Being the soldier and expert he was, one would have expected him to concentrate on matters of defence. Particularly at that time when the fortifications he had himself assessed were nearing completion. But it was not so. Having arrived after an abortive election for the council he found the battle between the politically minded was still on. He did not keep back, and was soon dispensing his ability to help what problems could be solved. In the process he could not help getting to know of the Maltese ultimate aim to obtain a more liberal constitution than they had.

There were of course the limits to which he could go. But here he was also fortunate in having Gerald Strickland enter politics in his time. Strickland was a young man of 25, born in Malta of Commander William Strickland and his Maltese wife, who came from a noble family. Young Gerald was educated in England where he took a legal degree at Cambridge. Also being elected President of the Cambridge Union in the process which marked him for a political career. Indeed he launched himself through the columns of the local press, both English and Maltese and it did not take him long to win a seat on the Council. Being on the reformist side it is surprising how he attracted the sympathy of Dr Fortunato Mizzi, the leader of the anti-reformists. And there could not have been a better team to be sent to London and the Secretary of State with the Council's proposals for a legislative assembly for Malta as all were hoping for.

Simmons continued to ride the storm. But he was also using his many skills in Malta's benefit wherever he could find the chance. Being an engineer he was soon planning and building a badly needed Poor House. And through his administrative abilkities he reformed many a charitable institution. He also found means to effect further reforms at the Customs and Postal departments, as well as the Lunatic Asylum. These might all have been little things. There was a much bigger assignment to confront him in pursuing the imminent change that he could feel was coming. And he lost no chance to do his bit. Not wanting to rest on despatches he went over to London and consulted the Secretary of State whenever he felt the need, and doing his utmost to keep him well informed on the Italian language question and all the other details that had to be known before the request made for a legislative assembly could be considered. More than the Secretary of State he was in contact with Joseph Chamberlain the Colonial Secretary, who had become the most important member of the Cabinet after having raised the prestige of his department which hitherto had been regarded as of minor importance.

Simmons' term was one of devotion to duty. Which comprised taking cognisance of the real Malta where this was lacking. And he succeeded. In London and elsewhere, the true image of the island and her people emerged. Except at the Union Club in Valletta where the clique continued with its attitude. And if a proof was ever needed that theirs was something more than simple arrogance there was the *faux pais* when the club black balled Sir

Adrian Dingli to refuse him membership. This was the most extreme limit of their folly which stunned all those who knew of it. Simmons included. He had harped on their foolishness since 1877. Now, to show this resent, he resigned his membership of the club. And so did the Duke of Edinburgh.

In 1886 the Duke was appointed Commander-in-Chief in the Mediterranean and this brought back the Duchess for another stay in Malta. But maybe there was a bigger impact made by the appearance of Prince George who was later to become King George V. He was a young lieutenant on *HMS Thunderer* and what is said of his popularity when ashore is confirmed by what was reported about his parents being worried with his stays in Malta with her gossip and coffee houses. Indeed there were soon to be rumours of some attachment to Culine Seymour, an admiral's daughter.

On 16th April, 1887 Malta was given a new constitution. Not exactly as had been proposed, but it gave the elected members a majority over those nominated. For the first time ever the people's representatives in the Council were having the power to legislate on most internal matters and also control the finances. The British Government retained only the right of intervention to be exercised only in exceptional circumstances.

It looked like a fitting climax to the many years of endeavour. Fitting too that it had to come in the year of Queen Victoria's Jubilee which was also being celebrated by the Maltese, who in commemoration erected a statue to their Queen close to the Governor's Palace in Valletta. It was also to be expected that one of the first proposals to be made by Simmons to the new Council would concern the military forces. In fact it was through his proposal that there was formed The Royal Malta Regiment of Militia on 1st May, 1889. Under the same arrangement the Royal Malta Fencible Artillery had its name changed to Royal Malta Artillery, which was to make much glory for its men in the future.

When his term was up Simmons left. Satisfied to leave Malta better than he had found her. And convinced that the new constitution would work well.

But it didn't. Because of the squabbles that ensued. Mostly political. Gerald Strickland became Chief Secretary in 1887 and for seven years tried to get things going. Proposing more harbour facilities, new industries, trade and agriculture. He even thought of creating a free port at Malta and starting a tourist trade. But everything involved money, and the council remained adamant, indeed becoming suspicuous, where expenditure was involved. Even proposals for essential services like the water supply and drainage were bludgeoned. Free education was short circuited because of the language question which had by now become like a cancerous growth to all Malta's chances of development.

Even more worrisome were the frequent resignations from the Council of men who could have saved it. And now in 1898 there had arisen the Hewson case, concerning Colonel J.L. Hewson who was coerced by the Maltese Courts to sign a statement of evidence taken in Italian which he did not understand. At a time when Chamberlain's temper was mounting in pace with the news of every controvesial step from the elected members of the Council, culminating with their rejection to amend the law whereby any English speaking person would have any sentence or decree delivered to him in English, but would be registered in English and Italian.

The fat was now in the fire, and Chamberlain was not prepared to accept this rejection. The amendments to the Criminal Laws were made by an Order in Council. But this was not all. Contrary to previous declarations that were made, Chamberlain now also directed the governor to proclaim that it was Her Majesty's Government's intention to substitute English for Italian in all legal proceedings after a period of 15 years.

This acted like a spark to a powder keg. Bringing protests and recriminations, and also a crisis to what should have been a benevolent conclusion to the Victorian period. It brought also new divergencies. Between Britain and Malta, as well as between the local politicians themselves. The man in the street could not follow and much less understand what was happening. And with this ignorance being bliss, it would have been a folly to be wise.

After all the likely outcome was loud and clear for all those who could see it. Politically the constitutional clock had been put back more than fifty years. Malta was back in the cul-de-sac of 1849, from which nothing and no one could foretell when it would emerge.

CHAPTER VI

MALTESE PAWN ON BRITAIN'S CHESSBOARD

In the quiet of his room at the Palace of San Anton, Lord Grenfell had sat hunched in his favourite chair reading the morning paper. Indeed he was only skimming through it. Now he put it aside impatiently and rose up. Dragging his feet he shuffled towards a window and looked with unseeing eyes at the beautiful gardens below him. With their flower terraces and orange groves all set into parallel fragments separated by walls covered by multi-coloured Bougannvillaea. He made a fine figure in his ceremonial uniform, and there was a good deal of the Bismarck in his appearance. But this morning there was something which was annoying him.

Anyone who knew him would have said it was unusual for him to put away a newspaper without reading it from beginning to end. With his being a very methodic person and of a firm will. But Grenfell himself would surely have answered, had he been asked, that he should have been reading the speech he was expected to deliver in an hour's time rather than the paper. His audience was to be made of the Parish Priests of Malta, who would be assembling as they had always done on Candlemas Day since the times of the Knights to present a candle to the ruler of the country. In the Order's time it had been a Grand Master to receive the candle. Since the British occupation it was the Governor. And this was going to be Grenfell's first occasion, after having been in office for just over a month.

He had been very glad to accept his appointment. Malta had held many sweet memories for him. It was only after he had arrived in the island on 6th January, 1899 that he realised the difficulties he would have to face. And rather than trying to sort them out in his own way he had paid a lightning visit to London to hear the worst from Chamberlain himself. The Colonial Secretary had told him of the council of government which was not following any concerted policies, and of the people who had retaliated vehemantly to the threat of substituting English for Italian. He had hinted at the possibility of intervention which could even withdraw the new constitution. If this were to be done then it would be like putting the island's constitutional clock back more than fifty years. It wasn't the kind of talk from which to elucidate his speech to the Parish Priests. What they woudl want to hear would be about progress and work.

Indeed there had been one encouraging hint given by Chamberlain about the expected bigger part Malta would have to play in an envisaged drastic stepping up of the naval construction programme. And this had led to preoccupation about her Grand Harbour being wde open and at the mercy of a stormy sea which could roll straight in to the discomfort of the fleet. This was not all. There was also the vulnerability of ships at anchorage to the new torpedoes that had been developed and which could be fired from outside the harbour. There were therefore plans in the offing for the construction of a breakwater to hold the rough sea and also to prevent any direct sight shots into the anchorage. This would serve as well to provide much needed work. But these plans were premature. And how could he hope to put something positive like this in his speech when he knew of the negative that was bound to preceed it?

He was relieved when there was a knock on the door and his ADC came in.

"Your coach is ready, Excellency," he said.

"All right. I am coming," replied Lord Grenfell.

He remained alone enough to damn himself for worrying too much. And also those who looked at constitutions with sanctimonious reverence to deem them like the ark of the covenant. Too sacred to be touched. During his run to the city he saw the sweating farmers working in their fields. Masons were chipping the white Malta stone in a blazing sun. One who recognized his coach doffed off his cap in salute. In the built up areas there were the herdsmen milking their goats from door to door and the hawkers plying their wares to appraising haggling housewives. On approaching Valletta he could not help glancing nostalgically at the Grand Harbour beneath him. There were more warships than he could care to count, and an even bigger number of boatmen with their multi-coloured *dgħajsas* plying from ship to ship and vice versa. He knew about them and their hard but steady work when the fleet was in harbour which also provided more swill to trade in as a sideline. He could also see the ant-like figures of men toiling at the dockyard which he realised must have grown in size since his first stay at Malta. As indeed had grown in number the cute small bars along the shores of Senglea and Vittoriosa where barmaids entertained the crews of the fleet. He remembered his ADC telling him of the familiar names of some of them, all copied from English life, like so many other things in the Maltese scene.

These people did not make Malta. Maybe it could be said that they made only the part that was conceived, gestated and born by the Imperial side. There was then the other part made of the artisans, tradesmen, businessmen and the professionals. Also the priests, monks and nuns, too numerous for counting. He had already met many of them, noticing their quaint characters shining in their sense of simplicity and loyalty. But he could never find any resemblance or connection between them and the kind of people which featured in his talks with Chamberlain. He knew of course of the politicians who bore allegiance to none except their own idealogy and those who they believed or made out to represent. But they must have formed a minority which was far more detached from the mass that really made Malta.

The parish priests were all there waiting for him when he arrived at the Palace, in the Hall of St Michael and St George. Young and old, holding their candle as their ticket of introduction. He looked at the sea of solemn faces trying to guess in a momentary game their political loyalties. But if they had any, they were not showing them. With the presentation over and a word of greeting exchanged with each and every one, he came to the dreaded moment of his speech. Scraps and snippets of his morning's thoughts of preoccupation flashed across his mind. They sounded longer in memory than the strident voices that had exhonorated the sections of the population he had seen on the way. Then he launched himself, aiming at establishing a common ground of his being one of them because he knew Malta through a previous term of service. Emphasising that the occasion was therefore more like a meeting between friends than a ceremonial function he appealed for confidence to be shared to face what troubles may lie ahead. He thought that Chamberlain would not have been pleased to hear this. But damn him. This wasn't his show now. It was then he noticed the look on some of the faces before him as if they didn't understand his reference to knowing Malta before. Didn't they? So he capitulated and told them the whole story. How as a young officer in the 60th Rifles he had served in Malta and nearly lost his life. He had been swimming at night in preparation for a race on the\morrow, when hardly had he completed half the course that he was seized by an enormous octopus. Finding himself in difficulties he had yelled for help from an attending boat, and it was only when this reached him that the octopus flopped off and disappeared.

It wasn't the kind of story fit for the occasion. But it thawed the priests in front of him. He felt happier then, and could talk to them as if in a family conclave. He drew on the similarity of his need for help in that first precarious situation during his first stay at Malta. And the present one as her governor. On that first occasion he had called the attending boat. Now he was calling them who were the leaders of the people. Instead of hiding behind a mask of smiles and politeness he went straight to the point and the subject he had dreaded to talk about. His talk was now more vivid; his gestures less restrained. He was in a way like another priest who had suddenly found the key to his own heart.

In the days that followed he tried not to think about the outcome. Hoping his appeal had sunk in. The truth was that he was hoping for some sort of a truce. With niether side making any move. To bring calm which was the most important element in the prevailing situation.

He knew that this was a universal requirement with a very sick world. Britain was still ailing under a series of defeats suffered at war with the Boers in South Africa, and this had spurred Germany and other opponents of the liberal principles she stood for, to be more irritating. Britain had also drawn European antagonism by refusing to join others in their subversive policy against the United States during the Phillipine War, and this left her with only Italy as a friend. It could be that after paying scant attention to the language question seeing in it only an unimportant squabble, Britain was now seeing the political implications involved which could be dangerous. Either to her friendship with Italy, or even to her connexion to Malta altogether.

Whether or not Grenfell's strategem worked, there was no further Maltese reaction. The ball was in Britain's court after the Malese rejection of the proposed Ordinance for evidence to be done in English in the case of English speaking persons. However, Chamberlain did not take long to react and passed the Ordinance by an Order in Council. None could question this and the matter might have ended calmly had he stopped there. But he didn't. There was also the decision for Her Majesty's Government to substitute English for Italian in all legal proceedings in 15 years' time. And Grenfell was directed to issue the necessary proclamation.

This took the flame to the powder keg which brought many protests. From the Elected members of the Council and from the Advocates who were the ones mostly hit. But not from the general public, which seemed to prove to Lord Grenfell that he had been right in his assumptions that this was a matter belonging to a section of the population and not to the general Maltese. His belief was substantiated when Queen Victoria died on 22nd January, 1901, and he could not help commending the demeanour of the Maltese people in expressing sorrow for their queen

Wreaths covered her statue and business came to a standstill during the period of mourning which lasted till King Edward VII acceded to the throne. There was celebrating again when later Mafeking and Ladysmith were relieved in the South African War. Valletta was all beflagged to celebrate the British victory and bands paraded in the crowded streets of Valletta. When in the evening Lord Grenfell was watching all this on his way to the opera, the crowd unhorsed his carriage and dragged it through the streets amidst tumultous cheering.

Grenfell was not connected with any spectacular reforms during his term but he was very much involved with the harassing Italian language question, as no other previous governor had been. He was now following the battle which the Italianate element took right up to London. And Chamberlain was costrained to extend his 15 year limit to 20. But then he found rough seas when Italy joined the skirmish. The British Government could afford to ignore Malta. But not Italy which was its only ally. It had still to be an Irish Member of Parliament to harass Chamberlain and force him to retreat. On 28th January, 1902, in his address to the King's speech, the Colonial Secretary withdrew the controversial proclamation. Not in any deference to Malta, but to remove any Italian ill-feelings.

Now that the language question was put aside, however inconclusively, it was the turn of the 1871 Constitution to come under fire. Grenfell knew and understood how the tactics of the Elected members of the Council had put Britain on fire with righteous wrath. His only hope of finding someone who could help him put some sense in others disappeared when Gerald Strickland, who had by now been knighted, had to leave on being appointed governor of the Leeward Islands. There was only one last effort he could make. To take the bull by the horns and speak to the people involved.

"Unless you change your tactics you will be forcing His Majesty's Government to modify your constitution," he told them. "You must remember as well that while your tactics are seen as the whims of a minority, the Constitution is a trust belonging to all the Maltese people."

But his pleas fell on deaf and stubborn ears.

"By agitating," some of them replied, "we may regain all the liberties we have lost. Let us therefore continue to do so and we shall win." But Grenfell knew they would lose. He had seen it done before. Had heard it justified with the cynicism of trouble makers as a normal political operation. When it might have been something else. His only wish now was to be away before it happened. And this was granted to him.

Against all expectations his successor, Sir Charles Mansfield Clarke had a very auspicious beginning. He arrived in time to welcome King Edward VII to Malta on 16th April, 1903. There was nothing to indicate that Malta was not the most stable and wonderful country in the world. With a popular monarch like Edward VII calling her so amidst the pageantry and gaiety of the celebrations. He laid the foundation stone of the breakwater which indeed promised prosperity to the country. On the Royal Malta Regiment of Militia he conferred the title of King's Own. And the people rejoiced like children and applauded until he left on the 21st.

Three days later the Elected Members of the Council were back with their attitude of harassment to refuse approval to the Education votes. This was the limit, but Chamberlain took a little longer. The votes were returned for their approval, but this time with the threat of proclaiming a new constitution if they were not approved. The Elected Members still refused. So on 22nd June, 1903, the 1887 Constitution was withdrawn.

And Malta was back in the *cul-de-sac* of fifty years back.

Soon after that June of 1903 the tide began to turn. Imperceptibly at first, like a page being turned to close a chapter on a generation of constitutional evolution, and open another on the navy and defence. Now launched by the starting of the work on the breakwater which was soon gathering steady momentum. Every available local man was taken on. And there soon had to be imported foreign labour as well. There began to come days when those who did not work would spend hours on the bastions watching to see the monstrous project taking shape. But to fill the time there was also the fleet in harbour now growing in strength as the pace of naval construction quickened. For those who could follow what was going on away from Malta's shores there was the news of the debate in London on naval policy in the Mediterranean.

It seemed that as if by a wave of a magic wand Britain had changed what Maltese inclinations there had been for political squabbling into what pertained to the naval fortress. Indeed, either because of the continued presence with its great fighting ships in harbour, or because of its personnel being always free with their spending on return to port, the Royal Navy was the more popular of the services. And as there had been the learning of British customs, dress, social behaviour and also the popular football, there was now the understanding of naval terms and jargon. Many could now tell the difference between a battleship, cruiser and a destroyer. Those who didn't, soon adapted themselves to call the three of them a gunboat. Every seaman was called Jack, a peaked cap meant a PO, and the officers got a Sir.

The loss of the Constitution of 1881 seemed to have affected only the diehards. And these were still making comparisons with what was happening in England as if to exonerate their attitude. They found little for their purpose in the Budget Crisis and the Abolition of the Lords' Veto that were going on at that time, but they were soon whooping with joy at the activities of the Vote for Women movement in that country. The government had not heeded it until it had carried its campaign in a sober constitutional way. It was only now in 1905 that it attracted the wanted attention after its members had smashed shop windows, threw inflammable material into post boxes, burned down public buildings, invaded the House of Commons and attacked Ministers with dog-whips and red pepper. If British women could do all that, any man could do it and even more, anywhere. Could this have been a lesson in retrospect? But if this was time for kindling fires they were soon being smothered by Chamberlain himself who went to Malta in 1907, obviously with such a purpose in mind.

More than this he made a hit. It had been his wish to see Malta for many years, he said, during a dinner given in his honour, and what he saw confirmed all that was said of the history and traditions of the small island. He had also a good word for Malta's place in the British Empire, calling her as one of its most important fortresses and which did not belong to Britain by right of capture or discovery. But by Maltese free will to ask for British protection. "The British fleet and Malta were complementary to each other," continued to say Chamberlain, "without the fleet Malta would be deprived of her glory and prosperity, but without Malta, the fleet would be without a haven and home to come to."

Maybe the climax in Chamberlain's visit came when Dr Fortunato Mizzi in a speech full of passion called the occupation of Malta a political enslavement. Chamberlain's reply was that he had never seen anyone who reminded him less of a slave than the honourable gentleman.

For the first time ever too, in the absence of the Lieutenant Governor Edward March Merewether, a Maltese Camillo Gatt who was the Auditor General, was made to act in his stead. Then towards the end of the year, there was Winston Churchill, the Under Secretary of State for the Colonies himself visiting Malta like a fairy god-mother to pat backs and suggest letting bygones be bygones. He even proposed that a request could be made for the constitutional status to be reviewed. This was ostensibly the British lion licking the mouse that had pulled its tail. It seemed that the pendulum which had swung forth to hit Malta was now swinging back again. What was the scope behind it?

Could this be found anywhere in the division of Europe with Germany forming the Triple Alliance with Austria and Italy while France joined with Russia to leave Britain isolated between the two continental animosities? Indeed, after British setbacks in the Boer War, there had been a German spurt which the Emperor had said would not stop until Germany would have an overwhelming superiority on the British Navy. In reply to Admiral Fisher's super-battleship the *Dreadnought* which could outrange and outsteam anything afloat, Germany had began building her own, and a race had started which could easily end in a war.

Prince George had now succeeded to the throne of England as King George V, carrying with him rumours about his time in Malta, where, a journalist by the name of Mylius wrote that the King, had married Culine Seymour, the Admiral's daughter. This painted him as a bigamist, and Mylius was prosecuted for libel which got him 12 months imprisonment. Even the Maltese Crown Advocate General, Sir Vincent Frendo-Azzopardi gave evidence in the libel case. It was a lie which had persisted for 20 years. But the case now stopped all melicious tongues. It also curbed what assumptions were being made in regard to a Maltese lace maker with whom Prince George was closely acquainted. At the right time she had borne a child who was then, as he was still in his manhood, a spoilt image of the king.

British Malta had not yet experienced a shooting war, and with all the forts bristling with unfired guns, the multi-coloured regiments, and her harbour crowded to its seams with magnificent fighting ships the word spelt adventure. The highlight was reached in 1912 after Winston Churchill became First Lord of the Admiralty to quicken the debate on naval policy which even to a beginner smacked of preparation of war. There were arguments galore from all sides of Parliament about the balance of power to be retained. And Malta was the focal point in all of them. Churchill was of the opinion that Malta's six battleships should be transferred to the Home Fleet to obviate any initial German attack, others said that there should be 12 and not six battleships at Malta.

This led to a meeting of the powerful Committee of Imperial Defence being held in Malta in May 1912 which was attended also by Lord Kitchener who went to the island on purpose and complemented his visit by inspecting her defences. In his arguments Winston Churchill was supported by the *Dreadnought*'s creator Admiral Sir John Fisher and after a very heated meeting their plan prevailed over all the others. The 4th Battle Squadron at Malta was to be moved to Gibraltar to be closer to Home waters, while Malta was to have four armoured cruisers and fifteen destroyers. The dockyard was to be maintained at top scale. Fort St Angelo wsa to be used as a base ship for the fleet instead of *HMS Egmont* which was towed back to England, and the fort took its name. The fort was therefore rated as a man-of-war. With its storeys becoming 'decks' and its rooms 'cabins', all under the command of a Flag Captain who had his quarters in the house of the governor at the top.

So much was said and written about Malta in those days as Britain was preparing for war. But not a word was mentioned about her inhabitants and their safety. There was only Admiral Troubridge who had occasion to write about the Maltese, saying that they were excitable and unreliable in war. Thirty years after, however, the world was to know how wrong he was.

Britain had in the meantime negotiated an *Entente Cordiale* with France with a gentleman's agreement to support each other in case of an attack by a third party. But then in June 1914 the Archduke Francis Ferdinand, heir to the Austrian throne was murdered in Sarajevo. Austria demanded humiliating penance from the Serbian Government which was not made in full. So Austria declared war on Serbia. Russia immediately came in to support Sebia while Germany supported Austria, and France backed Russia against Germany, all within the space of a few days. Britain was not obliged to join in the war, but when the situation was still in the balance news came that the Germans were attacking France through Belgium. This was it. An ultimatum was delivered to Germany demanding the immediate evacuation of Belgium, which expired at midnight on 4th August, 1914. And from that moment Britain was at War. And so was Malta.

CHAPTER VII

THE GREAT WAR 1914/18

War. The word appeared in bold lettering in every newspaper headline on that day of 5th August, 1914. It was also on every Maltese mouth. Without anybody really knowing what it signified.

British war orders issued a year before had laid down that if Britain were to find herself alone against the Triple Alliance, she would abandon the Mediterranean and concentrate on Gibraltar. But in al other cases the concentration would be at Malta. And so it was to be, with France fighting on Britain's side. "When the French Admirals discussed their plan of action at Whitehall," said Winston Churchill, "and agreed on basing the French Fleet at Malta, it could not be helped being remembered that this was the same island for which the British had fought Napoleon a little more than a century before." The French general must have turned in his grave.

Many were expecting thrills. And indeed the first one had come a few days before. When it was known how *HMS Inflexible* and *HMS Indefatigable*, two battlecruisers added to the Mediterranean fleet because of the presence of the German battle cruiser *Goebon* and the light cruiser *Breslau*, had while escorting French transports, met the German warships. But as Britain had not yet declared war, they did not engage them, and lost a golden opportunity never to repeat itself. In a way it was also a disappointment, and the Admiralty had relieved Admiral Sir Berkeley Milne of his command of the fleet, and Rear Admiral Troubridge took over in his stead.

If more thrills were wanted then they could be found locally in the days that followed. With the arrival of the French fleet in Malta, and the hectic activity of the mobilisation of the fortress that followed. There was the proclamation of martial law, the issue of paper currency, and the deployment of troops to their war positions. Severe censorship was also imposed. Then all warlike activity suddenly stopped, and those in search of thrills and news had to content themselves reading about what was happening in Belgium and France where a British Expeditionary Force was already fighting the Germans.

Things were not going well for the British forces so all regular garrison battalions in Malta were called to the front with the exception of two, The West Kent Regiment and the Northumberland Fusiliers remained, together with two London regiments which were temporarily for training as well as five hundred Maoris. The principal share for the defence of the island was left to the Royal Malta Artillery with a strength of 1,032 officers and men, and two battalions of the King's Own Malta Regiment with a strength of 3,393.

There was much Maltese despondency because of the outcome of the situation; however, many were more disappointed when as weeks and months of inactivity went past it began to seem to them as if Malta was forgotten in the tide of new events. What they did not know was that this kind of lassitude that followed was all in line with British plans. To reserve and maintain strength until it would be known on whose side uncommitted Italy would jump. Because if she were to join the enemy, then Malta would overnight find itself at the front, with her being only 60 odd miles from the Sicilian mainland.

But if the British acquiesced in this kind of respite they had not taken into consideration the Maltese, whose character had as ever brought unity in face of a common enemy. And the British war became also their own. They were far from being excitable and unreliable as Rear Admiral Troubridge had written about them some time before. Instead they preferred to get into the thick of it, and if the enemy did not go to them they would then go to him. It was in this spirit that the King's Own Regiment of

Militia requested, more than just volunteered, for foreign service. And its request was granted. On 14th January, 1915 its first battalion and a detachment of the second under Lieutenant Colonel Charles Sciortino left for Cyprus which was soon to be involved in the fighting that was to erupt at the Dardanelles.

In the absence of any organised recruiting there were soon to be individual Maltese soldiers finding or wangling their way to serve on the front. A number of officers from the Maltese regiments got themselves attached to British units to fight both in France and Gallipoli, and not less then eight of them were awarded the Military Cross, some of them posthumously.

But Malta was not destined to remain idle, and when the Allies began operations at the Dardanelles, however indirectly, she became involved. The first naval bombardment of the Gallipoli peninsula had proved fruitless. When the fleet went in again it steamed into newly laid Turkish minefields. One French battleship, the *Bouvet* and three British, the *Inflexible, Irresistable* and *Ocean* were sunk. This seemed to set the shape of things to come, and the casualities that were to be expected. Malta was asked whether it could provide hospital accommodation. The request coincided with the arrival in Malta of the new Governor, Field Marshal Lord Methuen in February 1915 who immediately threw himself body and soul into turning the island into a rear base for the theatre of operations. The harbours and dockyard needed no push. They were more than busy with French and British warships as well as troop transports. Whether it was repair or refit they wanted it was quickly done; and stores and ammunition were found in abundance. Malta was back to the time of the Crimean War. Only that now all felt that they were closer to the battle which had somehow become their own. In the meantime, under the fostering guidance of Lord Methuen, hospitals were springing up like mushrooms. Barracks and schools were utilised. Any buildings that could house the thousands of beds that were arriving would do. Where no building was available there would have to be tents. There were finally in all some 27 hospitals.

On 25th April, 1915 British and Empire troops landed at Gallipoli under withering fire to suffer heavy losses in killed and wounded. There were not less than 38,000 British casualities in that operation. And on 4th May the first wounded began arriving at Malta. There were crowds in the streets as the wagons full of sick and crippled humanity passed along. They weren't the curious or busy-bodies. But men and women who were not engaged elsewhere, and felt they had to do their bit. Even if this was to cheer the wounded, and throw small comforts like cigarettes and sweets into the wagons as they went past. By the end of May there were already some 4,000 cases being treated in eight hospitals. Entailing the necessary medical and lay personnel who had to work round the clock.

Now there was the beginning of a new scare after the German submarine U309 torpedoed and sank the British battleships *Triumph* and *Majestic* in the Dardanelles. Even so, none could be bothered. There was work to be done. And those who weren't working were soon collecting money to organize entertainment for the wounded which kept increasing in number.

But this was far from being Malta's only contribution in the conflict. Ironically enough, France had been adamant to promote any of her Mediterranean ports as a vanguard lest the Austrian Fleet would bombard it. And Italy was similarily concerned. But Britain was very much aware she could not do away with such a fortress since she had to protect the vital sea routes through the Mediterranean. Both to the theatre of opertions at Gallipoli and to the Suez Canal. None would fit for this requirement more than Malta. By now the British fleet in the Mediterranean had grown to 15 battleships, 5 heavy cruises, 16 light cruisers, 16 monitors, 36 destroyers and 16 submarines. All of which were based there. This armada entailed also a respectable force of depot and repair ships. At this time too there was the first association with the name of *Ark Royal*, which was a seaplane carrier and joined the fleet at Malta.

For the first time it occurred to the Admiral Superintendent, then Vice-Admiral J.A. Limpus, that notwithstanding the spacious harbours to accommodate an armada of this size, the island was inadequately defended. This was to be confirmed by his successor Admiral G.A. Ballard. In particular there was the fact that only Grand Harbour was fitted with a boom defence. Ports like Marsamxett, Marsaxlokk and St Paul's Bay which were used as anchorages for both warships and merchantmen were open to submarine attack. It was a risk which could only be minimized by having motor launches patrolling the entrance of these ports. Then someone struck on the idea to place a line of buoys to bluff enemy submarines in thinking there was a minefield. It seems that the bluff worked since there was never any attack delivered in harbour.

There was also a chance for the many Maltese who, notwithstanding the fact that they were not in uniform, had hoped for the opportunity to serve on the front. When the call went out for labour to support the fighting forces in the Dardanelles, there were enough applicants to form a Maltese Labour Battalion of 1,000 men and 12 officers from the King's Own Malta Regiment of Militia who were quickly despatched to the battle area. When soon after there was a similar need at Salonika, the experiment was repeated and the required 800 men were found in no time. Both units remained in action till the end of the Daranelles campaign, by which time the number of sick and wounded in Malta had risen to 25,000 which earned the island the title of the Nurse of the Mediterranean.

This was in fact what Malta was getting in recognition of her endeavours. A lousy slogan, her people thought, to be recorded in history books for posterity. Not that anyone expected anything. But there was more than a stray thought or even a simple feeling that no more tangible recognition would be forthcoming Neither in money nor in kind. The workers at the dockyard in particular, now risen to 14,000 from the normal 3,500, all had families and wanted to live. Nothwithstanding the increased volume of work, the cost of living had increased out of proportion to wages. There was also the occasional occurrance that would flash a reflection of old days with two ways and measures being adopted for equivalent persons doing the same work. Depending only whether one was British or Maltese. It had been hoped all along that the war would remove all this. But then there was always the consolatory thought that the war had not yet ended.

Indeed it hadn't. And to emphasize this there was the submarine menace which far from decreasing had grown to unexpected proportions. By the end of 1915 there had been some 15 German U-Boats operating in the Mediterranean. And as if to confirm the reality of this menace there was now one of them torpedoing and sinking *HMS Russel* with 200 of her crew on 27th April, 1916, just three miles off Malta. Her sister ship *Cornwallis* suffered the same fate 60 miles south east of the island. It seemed to the Admiralty then that with all the anti-torpedo nets, hydrophones and anti-submarine mines that were introduced, the German U-Boats were still getting the upper hand. More than the escorts that were being provided, now also strengthened by a flotilla of Japanese destroyers, there should be those who would seek the submarines wherever they may be. Then someone thought of the Royal Flying Corps. Yes, why not? A seaplane could go farther and faster than any ship to find or attack a submarine. A seaplane base would certainly help the situation in the Mediterranean. And where could it be located other than in Malta? Work was taken in hand immediately to construct a seaplane shed and a slipway at Kalafrana. The second stage would follow when these were ready with having a Dockyard Construction Unit transferred there to set up and assemble aircraft from components which would be sent from the United Kingdom.

But dockyard workers were occupied with something else. The Admiralty had finally consented to grant an increase of 10% to their weekly wage. It sounded good until one knew that the weekly wage was ten shillings. It was considered inadequate and therefore not acceptable. But what could one do? Then someone asked what would have British workers done had this happened in their country? But it had happened there, said those who knew. And there were soon the self appointed speakers to tell all of the British Trade Union Movement that had taken a revolutionary turn only a few years back.

"The Unions had been disappointed that the newly emerged Labour Party had not done more for the working classes," the speakers said, "and some of the younger and wild spirits among the leaders began to preach a return to the gospel of social revolution as taught by Karl Marx."

But this wasn't what the Maltese workers wanted to hear. They did not understand what was a trade union, and none of them knew about Karl Marx. All they wanted to know was what had British workers done to get their dues. They had heard of strikes.

"Of course there were strikes," they were told. "There had been the great railway strike in 1911, because the companies would not recognise the right of the Unions to speak for the workers. Then followed a gigantic miners' strike to enforce a minimum wage all over the country of five shillings a day."

"And we are only asking for something more than our lousy ten shillings a week," some shouted.

Then they were told hoiw over a million men were idle in that strike which affected other industries and struck a blow at the coal export trade.

"In the same way as we would effect the war effort if we go on strike now," said someone.

And his words were a new revelation of the strength existing in a united worker. And a first lesson in industrial relations. So on 7th May, 1917 the dockyard workers went on strike, which was the first one in Malta.

This was an unexpected contratemps for the British authorities in Malta, who might have never expected it from the workers who had been docile (they might have called it servile) for more than a hundred years and under worse conditions. But missing the point that all this time had also been one of learning. Even now when faced with this sudden development, an agitated Admiralty reacted badly. While the strikers just stayed away from work the authorities closed down all docks and depots and placed soldiers to guard them. They also called out troops to help the civil power. When it was known that on the 9th the strikers intended marching into Valletta, they sent machine gun detachments to the Palace Square. But they needn't have lost their heads. The strikers marched into Valletta and even spoke to the Governor and the Archbishop but without provoking anyone. If there was anything which

108

might have been of any provocation it was the presence of the machine-gunners pointing their weapons at the people who had served them and their country blindly for more than a century.

That same evening the Admiral Superintendent promised the strikers that if they were to return to work on the following day, he would submit their grievances to the Lords of the Admiralty in London. And the workers, being the sensible people they were, agreed So they returned to work on the following day. And Rear Admiral Ballard kept his word and went to London on their behalf. As a result, their wages were increased by 50%.

With this matter satisfactorily settled, feelings and tempers quietened down. But their effect was not erased. Even if there were the British olive branch being proferred when the Archbishop was knighted for his conciliatory efforts. There began now to be generated new thoughts, bringing back aspirations which had been placed in cold storage by the war. As a reminder of the still existing language question, however dormant, there was now Dr Enrico Mizzi who had inherited the ideals of his dead father Dr Fortunato Mizzi. He had been elected to the Council in 1915 and was a stormy petrel right from the very start. But now, on 29th March, 1917 he had thrown all caution to the wind and condemned the British Government with terms which bordered on sedition. Coming so soon after the dockyard upheaval this might have shown the British a red light and without further ado, Dr Mizzi was arrested and court-martialled to be condemned for one year's imprisonment. With an obvious lesson meted out by a determined British Government it was left to the Governor to change the sentence to one of a severe reprimand. And as this drama was going on, the Maltese were only silent spectators. Those with anti-reform ideas being apprehensive of a new British attitude seemingly intent to combat their cause. The rest were glad and satisfied with the turn of events. They might have been prone to react themselves, but there was still a war on which made them bury their differences.

The only warlike dangers to the Mediterranean were now coming from mines and submarines, and with Maltese efforts having seemingly lost their previous importance, it was more than poetic justice to have all minesweeping operations entrusted to them. The Malta Minesweeping flotilla was now by mid-1917 being manned by Maltese ratings and officered by the British. The submarine menace was also being attended to, with the Dockyard Construction Unit at Kalafrana now fast assembling aircraft from components. With the Royal Air Corps having combined to form the Royal Air Force there was then born at Kalafrana in June 1918 the Royal Air Force Malta Group. It was placed under the command of Colonel A.M. Longmore who was later to become Air Chief Marshal Sir Arthur Longmore. In August 1918 this group had No. 267 (Seaplane) Squadron with F2A flying boats and No. 268 Squadron equipped with Short Sunbeam 320 float seaplanes. To continue operations whenever the sea was rough and aircraft unable to take off, there was constructed a temporary landing slip at the racecourse at Marsa which was equipped with two DH9 aircraft. But more than for the service it was to render, this group became significant by marking the beginning of a long and happy association between Malta and the Royal Air Force.

There was now nothing else to be done until the war would end. And the Maltese were praying to God for a happy outcome. They could not help knowing of the wiping out of a British Army in France, and the German push that was making the Allies withdraw mile after mile. In truth their hearts went out with every stroke of the bad news. But their prayers kept rising in unison full of their characteristic hope. It was now the only contribution they could make for their battle, and they did it wholeheartedly. Irrespective of any idealogical differences.

With the coming of September there were new movements in the Allied command. All troops were placed under Marshal Foch, while American forces were hastened to go into action. To laymen and strategists alike these were moves of desperation. The last tremors of a dying man, some called them. But they weren't. Rather than rallyng, they divided the Germans. Revolutions broke out in Germany now that the people were unable to endure more of the privations they had to suffer. Their navy mutineed and the Kaiser fled. French, American and British armies began to advance, side by side, and driving the enemy back throughout September, symbolically egged on by millions of allied voices raised in hope and cheer. Amongst them, no doubt, being those of Maltese throbbing hearts and prayers. Then, with Bulgaria and Austria already collapsed, Germany surrendered.

The 11th November, 1918 was a day like any other in Malta. But with the news of the ceasefire, the autumn leaden skies seemed to burst with newly found sunshine. The long silent churchbells began clanging, and ships in harbour were sounding their sirens. Pandemonium broke loose to rouse town, village and suburb. Everywhere people were emerging out of doors hugging and kissing each other. The celebrations that were quickly mounted by thousands of willing hands kept going right into the night. And nobody worried about the morrow. That, notwithstanding everything, they were convinced would be another day.

CHAPTER VIII

A CRUCIAL AFTERMATH

It was all over bar the shouting. But this was soon over too. To be followed by a deep silence like the sudden stopping of a clock. And hearts were all at a loss on coming in confrontation with the immediate unknown future.

There was a breathing space in Britain however when for some time after the cessation of hostilities there continued to be an artificial boom. Business was brisk as before, for there was still some money about, and the supply of consumer goods was insufficient to meet the demand. This, however, did not delude the coalition government that took over. After all, even if there was for a time enough food for everyone the country was still plagued with a high cost of living which rather than finding its level continued to soar. There was a shortage of houses, and returning ex-servicemen began to find it difficult to get employment. The same situation prevailed in Malta. Only that she had no boom, and therefore no respite. In Britain too, trade unions which had gained strength during the war were now planning to exhort higher wages than ever before and in what way they could, try to maintain improved standards of living. These did not exist in Malta.

What might have raised Maltese hopes was the national feeling in the United Kingdom which has been one of the main causes of the war. This was now being intensified rather than allayed and reflecting on the empire where it was being sensed there was the beginning of nationalistic aspirations. The big members, already being referred to as "daughter nations" were immediately placated and they could send their delegates to the Paris Peace Conference in the first half of 1919 from which there was later to emerge the League of Nations. But in other parts of the empire what aspirations there were went unnoticed and this could only lead to bitter struggles. Amongst them there was Malta.

To counteract the sudden increase in unemployment because of the return of jobless ex-servicemen, the governor Lord Methuen thought of a crash plan for emigration. Searching for a country which would take thousands, he thought of the new dominion of Australia where conscription had been adopted and was denuding the already low labour force. He sent 96 emigrants straight-away to pioneer a bigger flow. But they were soon the cause of a hue and cry by anti-conscriptionists which led to the immediate withholding of further emigrants. The United Stats too had similarly prohibited illiterate immigrants which automatically closed doors to most of the Maltese.

It is true that Lord Methuen did not give up and he tried to introduce more possibilities for education, while he quickly appointed an Emigration Commission to find the necessary outlets. These were all meritorious steps. But they also needed time, which was in the meantime mounting up agitation for a seemingly complacent Britain to a Maltese situation. It had to be Maltese initiative to get things going and an already acclaimed patriot, a lawyer Dr Filippo Sciberras, stepped into the breach. He was entrusted with calling a meeting of representatives from constituted bodies to form a Maltese National Assembly. The idea was to request and bring pressure on Britain to grant Malta a new form of government, more in harmony with the principles of the British Constitution. This, it was believed, would find the answer to all the problems ailing the country and which were becoming more precarious from day to day.

But even while this was going on, University students were already indulging in a rag along the streets of Valletta to protest against an intended change of degrees meant to substittue bachelorships for doctorates. And their behaviour

113

was not that orderly.

Admittedly things were moving, but beneath the polished surface of people ready to compromise and hoping for a reasonable British attitude there was a wider world where thousands of ordinary people wanted a job they could not find, also food and clothing they could not buy. Here the portents were not so rosy and the situation was becoming more explosive. From day to day Lord Methuen and the handful of people around him were hoping for a British Government reply, and a positive one to allay fears and suspicion. But with the days becoming weeks and these running into months, there was no decision from London. In the meantime small sectors already with their back to the wall were trying to improve their own particular situation. The teachers in government schools, for example, who had a princely salary of £8 per annum had reached the limit of their endurance. It was one of them in a Valletta school who incited the others to join him and ask for an increase. They agreed and made a petition. But who was to lead? So they appointed their signature in the form of a circle without a beginning or end. Indeed they needn't have had any fear for the Officer Administering the Government, deputizing for Lord Methuen who had left, realised their plight and authorised the requested increase. It was a breakthrough which was to be recorded in the pages of Maltese history for during discussions the teachers made bold and suggested the formation of a trade union. To their surprise they were told that there would not be any objection to this. Like them the Admiralty Maltese Clerks formed their trade union as a branch of the British Civil Service Association, to be followed by the Maltese Civil Service clerks in forming their own.

Even while this was going on which gave Malta her first trade unions, there was the British reply shifting the onus of recommending a change of the Constitution or otherwise on the new governor who was shortly to fill the place vacated by Lord Methuen. It was the kind of diplomatic reply to keep people guessing and hoping, which did curb what wrath had accumulated in those who had reached the limit. The general worker had not seen any attempt at

114

improvement, as the white collar workers had done. Instead he had to face unemployment and soaring prices which he could not afford. Now also that of bread which was the main staple of the poor man's diet. His battle had become more like a personal feud, and therefore a dangerous powder keg.

The dreaded spark was applied on 7th June. It began with a crowd of youths who coverged on Valletta in the morning before the Assembly was due to meet at the Governor's Palace. The rowdy elements forced shopkeepers to close their shops, and this being what had been done by university students during previous rags seems to indicate that the students were behind this disturbance too. A police sergeant trying to infuse some order was manhandled. He escaped minus his helmet which was soon being kicked about by the crowd like a football. When the crowd reached the governor's palace, it found the door closed. It was now that it was incited to violence and those who had until then been only protesting hotheads now became rioters. They rushed to the University where they tore down the Union Jack from where it was hoisted then proceeded to wreck the laboratory and library, throwing furniture in the street and setting fire to it. This again implicating the student element that must have been with the crowd. It was then the turn of the pro-British newspaper *Malta Daily Chronicle*, and its offices were ransacked. So were the homes of pro-British politicians and mill owners. Troops from the West Yorks Regiment were called out to control the situation, and when attacked by the rioters they opened fire killing three and wounding another who died later.

It was the one and only occasion that Maltese blood was shed at British hands and this shocked everyone on both sides to be evidenced by the calm that seemed to follow. It was, however, an unnatural calm. More like an imposed truce. And even when the Officer Administering the Government, in the absence of the new governor not yet arrived, spoke to a deputation on the following morning and then addressed the crowds from the Palace balcony, agitation could still be noticed amongst his listeners. Indeed that same evening the rioters broke out again. This time their targets being the Union Club, the house of another mill owner, and a flour mill at Hamrun. Marines were then landed to control the situation while all troops were confined to barracks. Streets were patrolled while Valletta was paralysed. Dockyard, banks and shops were closed, while members of the clergy were at the fore to bring back calm, and the situation remained tense for a few days until Lord Plumer, the new Governor, arrived.

Coming straight from Germany where he had been in command of the Army of Occupation, he found a very strange albeit tense atmosphere. Streets guarded by troops, and top security arrangements. But he told his chauffeur to drive slowly, and then purposely stopped the car away from the Palace to afford him the chance to walk through the thousands of people on the main square in Valletta. There was neither fear nor apprehension as he walked unconcernedly through the crowds. Smiling and waving his hand in greeting without knowing if there was any acknowledgement. On arriving at the Palace he found the General Officer Commanding the Troops awaiting him, with a contingent of soldiers.

"What's this?" asked Lord Plummer.

"It's your guard, your Excellency," replied the GOC.

"How many are there?"

"Three hunded."

"Then march out all but twenty within ten minutes," ordered Lord Plumer.

And the execution of that order was the first act that morning to unspring some of the tension that was on everyone. It was not what one might have expected in the way of showmanship. Lord Plumer meant business and rather than hearing about the situation from the people around him he quickly summoned a deputation to meet him within two hours of his arrival. He listened to all that was said and his comments were sympathetic but to the point. When the deputation left it felt more confident and calm.

The situation did not return to normal within the next few days. There were things to be done and measures to be taken. Like the admonishing of the students for their agitation, the imposition of censorship and the posing of troops at strategic points. All being in the way of prevention. There were also some arrests to be made. But as every move was being made calmly and purposely without raising any reaction, there were more people thinking of Lord Plumer as the ideal man for Malta. Every Maltese was seeing the new Governor's picture in the papers every day. Doing this and doing that. And everyone soon learned to recognise in his steadfast eyes the look of the gallant and determined leader that he was.

Notwithstanding the impact he had made which brought the wanted calm to the situation, Lord Plumer was well aware that nothing would suit the island he was sent to govern less than a self-government. Truly enough this was one of his terms of reference and he lost no time in making the appropriate recommmendations. But the Maltese did not know this. What they knew was that unless the situation was improved not even Plumer would save them. Even so, in the way of a booster to relieve the immedate situation, he introduced a bread subsidy and started a programme of public works. Civil Servants were also given a rise in salaries. This wasn't all, for his recommendtions were finding a positive response by the British Government and a few months later earned Malta a grant of £250,000.

As it was, a Britain similarily involved with Ireland and India could not ignore Malta. The more so that the whole economic life of Italy had now been thrown out of gear by the war and armed factions were heading for civil strife with an unknown outcome. So to assess the situation in Malta rather than settle it, there was sent L.S. Amery, the Under Secretary of State for the Colonies, in September. He found a ready made Maltese plan for a two house constitution worked out by the National Assembly which provided for a Legislative Assembly of elected members and a Senate of nominated members and others to be elected on a limited franchise within those movements to represent the nobility, clergy, chamber of commerce, trade unions and university graduates. He decided, however, that in the interests of both sides there should be two diarchies or systems of government. One dealing with local affairs and elected by the Maltese, and an imperial one to look after foreign affairs and defence. Both of these then were to be united in the Governor. This wasn't anything original but almost similar to what Britain had done for India. On 20th November, British official agreement to grant this kind of constitution was announced in the House of Commons and in the local Council of Government. As if to emphasize the haste now so evident in the process, on 3rd December the Secretary of State, Lord Milner, called at Malta to confirm the news in person.

"We are giving you the engine," he told the people, "it's up to you now to find the engineers."

And that was the signal which sent the politicians rushing to form their political parties.

The first in the field was Sir Gerald Strickland, who after his retirement from the Colonial Service in 1917 had returned to Malta. He quickly started going to form the *Anglo-Maltese Party* which was to have as its aim the pride in British Citizenship. But there was another party with similar aims of promoting pro-British interests in Malta being formed by Dr Augustus Bartolo under the title of *Constitutional Party*. On the other extreme to bolster the Italianate element there was Dr Enrico Mizzi laying the foundations of what he called *Democratic Party*. Then as if to lay a buffer zone between the two extremes there was a clergyman, Monsignor Panzavecchia to lead the *Unione Maltese*. All four parties were expected to represent Maltese opinion until then. But there was still a newcomer coming into the field with a new ideal to protect the underdog. This was to be the *Labour Party* and its sponsor was Lieutenant Colonel William W. Savona.

So while it was left to 1921 to see the actual emergence of the political parties, there were also in this year the many expectations for the approval of the final draft of the Constitution by the British Government. Opinions were varied with the majority being confident that Britain would now go ahead. There were those, however, who could not forget the many other occasions in the past when British opinion was shaken by what was assumed hardy protestant elements, particularly where the Maltese catholic religion was concerned. And as might have been done in the past there could now be some lobbying with the same scope. This could have been only imagination. As

King Edward VII laying the foundation stone of the Breakwater on 18th
April, 1903

The Foundation Stone

King Edward VII with Royal Family group at San Anton Gardens

HMS *Ramillies* in drydock at the dockyard

Monument for the fallen on 7th June, 1919

Duke and Duchess of York arriving at Main Guard in Valletta for their
visit from 17th to 21st June, 1927
(National Library of Malta)

Laying the foundation stone of Duke of York Avenue
(National Library of Malta)

there still was silly bothering by a handful for the Anglican St Paul's Church erected in Valletta in 1844 having retained the highest belfry, looking down on the score of domes of catholic churches in Valletta. As if this signified an element of dominance over them.

But indeed the constitution had a relatively smooth passage through parliament, with only two exceptions. One had to be the language question; but the other was indeed the clause laying down the catholic religion as the religion of Malta. This was changed to infer that all persons in Malta shall have full liberty of conscience and the free exercise of religious worship. Adding as well that none shall be excluded from holding any office because of his religious beliefs. And having no brief for what might have been attributed to them the Maltese accepted this. The language question was settled by having English and Italian as the official languages of Malta, but with English taking precedence in administrative matters and Italian to be used as a second language accompanying English texts. The Maltese language was to enjoy all such facilities as necessary, particularly as it was the language of popular intercourse. Italian, however, was retained in the Courts, but with resort to English being made with persons who did not understand Italian.

The Senate was to consist of 17 members with 2 representatives from the Nobility, University, Chamber of Commerce and Trade Unions, while the remaining nine were to be elected according to the rules of the class they represented. The Legislative Assembly was to have 32 members elected by the people through a system of proportional representation.

And that was that. Britain could now put the Constitution into force on 16th May, 1921, and let Malta do the rest while British attention could be diverted to other developments in the Mediterranean, particularly on Italy now with its business crippled and constant labour disputes accompanied by violence where the name of one, Benito Mussolini, was flashing like a meteor in the sky and lending hope to a finished nation. So as Malta went into its first election campaign with gusto, all out and convinced of settling once and for all her future existence, Italy was going through more troubled waters for her own. There were many Maltese eyes watching also that complicated situation and hearts might have throbbed with sorrowful palpitations. But Britain was watching both. For her the two situations had become locked in a race on which she had high stakes.

Sir Gerald Strickland had in the meantime found it convenient to amalgamate his party with that of Dr Augustus Bartolo taking the leadership himself but retaining the name of Constitutional Party for the two elements now fused into one. Dr Enrico Mizzi too changed his party's name to that of Democratic Nationalist. These were minor changes to the two factions which were considered to be the main contestants in the election. Even so, neither of them won that first election. It was the middle Unione Maltese which emerged with the largest single block of seats constituting a first problem for its leader, Monsignor Panzavecchia, who being a cleric could not very well become Prime Minister. So he stood aside to let Joseph Howard, OBE, to become the first Prime Minister of Malta.

The sun rose in an unusual fiery splendour on that autumn morning of 1st November, 1921. Crowds converged on Valletta like busy ant-like communities. From the early hours of the morning shopkeepers were closing their doors. This time quite willingly and not because of any coercion. But to find a convenient place at the Palace Square and witness the pageantry that was expected. A bigger crowd had already gone to the bastions round Grand Harbour now full of warships all dressed overall, with pinnaces fleeting from ships to shore as the important hour approached, but bringing back to onlookers the nostalgic look of a Malta which many had feared to have disappeared for ever. Now all knew it was coming back again, and thoughts must have flown to the Governor's Palace where the ceremony would soon be held to make this expectation a fact.

There was clapping and cheering as the ship bringing Edward, the Prince of Wales, entered Grand Harbour. It was him Britain had chosen to conduct on her behalf this momentous occasion. The tumultous cheering

120

accompanied him until he went ashore from where he proceeded to Valletta and the first meeting of Parliament he had to inaugurate. The pageantry soon shifted to the Palace where the Prince arrived to an equally tumultous reception by the people lining the streets and filling the main square. Then a fanfare of trumpets announced his arrival in the crowded and animated Hall of St Michael and St George. His speech then carried Britain's message endorsing Malta's utility as an impregnable fortress as it had always been since the beginning of the reign of his father King George V and through that of his grandfather King Edward VII. There had been occasions when this had seemed to lose importance, but the new Constitution was expected to bring that back and Malta would revert to her past glory, now to remain for ever. He then declared the Parliament open.

His declaration was followed by flourishing trumpets in the Hall, and the Royal Salute of the troops outside to be simultaneously accompanied by the cheering crowds. The warships in harbour fired salutes, and as the last shot echoed itself out there was the sound of churchbells pealing from every church in the island as every one in town and hamlet who could not be in Valletta that day joined in the rejoicing.

But the ceremony was not over yet. There was still a small but significant function the Prince of Wales had to carry out on behalf of his father. The conferring of the acolade on a much moved Dr Filippo Sciberras. The man who had been instrumental in bringing the Constitution to a successful conclusion. And his conferment was acknowledged by the cheering of all those present in the hall. Maltese and British. Both endorsing their respective recognition of his services. For a Malta which had now obtained self governing rights, and a grateful Britain perturbed by the news of a few days back of a Mussolini having formed the Fascist movement and marching on Rome to seize power by force.

Now Britain had in Malta something more than just a naval base. Even with a reduced Mediterranean fleet there were always enough ships of Admiral Sir John de Robeck's 4th Battle Squadron to activate the harbour. Battleships like *Iron Duke, Ajax, Benbow, Centurion, Emperor of India* and *King George V* found their permanent places along the main aisle of the harbour as if to become a part of the background. Six C Class cruisers and one destroyer flotilla of 23 ships found their home in the various creeks.

But the biggest impact was made by the crews going ashore on liberty. To be welcomed in the towns and cities around Grand Harbour with each party finding its own particular haunt. Whether this was an ordinary bar, club or even a private house. There were now more bars and entertainment places being made available with the traditional English names. Not only in the three cities of Vittoriosa, Cospicua and Senglea but also in Valletta where Strait Street became the mecca of a generation of British sailors and soldiers, and got the name of *The Gut* which stuck till these very days. Names like *Folies Bergere* and *The New Follies* were soon included with the dozens of murky night spots, contrasting sharply with Kate Meyrick's clubs in London which someone wanted to emulate.

This sudden influx of British manhood to a now agreeable Malta might have also given an impetus to dancing which in the United Kingdom had just become a public affair. This was now a madness which seized all classes, sharpening all appetites and at the same time depriving them of respect for tradition. The Charleston and the Black Bottom were for the first time being danced in Malta and spread like a prairie fire. Even though the gestures and attitudes of the dancers were so many echoes of the jungle for the Maltese. This life of dance halls and night clubs belonged of course to members of the British services. When they happened to penetrate into traditional Maltese places then they had to comply with the formalities and to accept the chaperones keeping surveillance of their wards which had been considered a duty of parents from time immemorial.

The more sophisticated could of course partake of Maltese top entertainment at the opera. Seasonal repertoires were held by the best Italian artists of the time at the Royal Opera House in Valletta. Evening dress then gave it a glamour it now lacks. British servicemen were now also more prone to welcome the prescribed Maltese *Festas* enlivened by lights, decorated churches, processions, loud fireworks and bands. These last musical groups showing and boasting of their banners with insignia and name of their club which very often was of British personalities of the time. There were bands and clubs dedicated to Queen Victoria, the Prince of Wales, the Duke of Edinburgh, the Duke of Connaught and others. As of course there was the King's Own Band which was, as it still is, one of the most important of them all.

But if this was making Britain look on Malta as some sort of a rest camp for her forces, the island was by a process of amalgamation becoming a second home to British servicemen. The Maltese could realize how they were adopting characteristics of the British who themselves were also being imbued with Maltese customs. For those who had brought over their families to Malta, the island became to them more like their first home. To the Navy and Army there was now added a small element of the Royal Air Force which was still operating seaplanes from Kalafrana on naval co-operation duties like spotting torpedo running, range finding and photographic reconnaissance. In January 1923, however, the first airfield was opened at Hal-Far to be used as a shore base by carrier aircraft, requiring more personnel for this third armed British service. Admittedly, families of the two nationalities did not meet much socially. After all there was the NAAFI to cater for the services who also had their own clubs. But whenever ships would leave harbour for exercises or some cruise there would now be the British housewives to mix with their Maltese counterparts on the bastions. For they had taken to that custom too. As if realizing how they belonged to the same family of their sunburnt neighbours to be together in calm and in crises.

★　★　★

A disturbance to a six years lull in 1924 did not come from Italy, where Britain had been watching the storm clouds gathering, but from Turkey which was making evident her intetions to attack Iraq. Britain was not involved, but was required by her commitments to the

League of Nations to intercept any Turkish aggressive action, if this were to materialise. The plan was for the Mediterranean fleet to occupy the Turkish Islands, enter the Sea of Marmora and blockade Costantinople. It was expected that in such an eventuality Turkey would mine the Dardanelles. Therefore what minesweepers had lain in reserve at Malta were quickly recommissioned. There was also a minesweeping flotilla brought over from England, while extra colliers were called in to support the fleet. Luckily the crisis fizzled out in 1926 and the fleet was made to stand down. It had been more like a false alarm. Creating that little extra work, and providing a training spin to the navy. Britain was soon back to her state of complacence. Little knowing of the trouble looming ahead.

It was the kind of trouble that needn't have arisen had Britain heeded the paradox in the local political situation. It had been there for everybody to see how notwithstanding the 120 year old British rule there had been no pro-British party elected to govern in six years during which there had been three elections. On each and every occasion there had been the *Unione Maltese* returned to power. Which was more of a middle way party. Neither too much inclined towards all that was British nor tied up to the Italianate extreme. And it had never occurred to anyone, it seems, that this was no normal situation. As if that deeper than the positive accrued during the occupation there was also negative element in the attitude of the occupiers. Not that strong maybe of swaying anyone to the opposite side, but enough to keep one aloof and in abeyance. As if the majority wanted to be British but was not yet sure it was accepted. But there seems to have been Britain's acquiscance to such a surmise as well. And never had British characterisation as a bulldog been so clearly demonstrated in all its sublime complacence.

It had to be the sudden thunderbolt of 1926 to shake her up. When the middle party *Unione Maltese* merged with the *Democratic Nationalists* to form the *Nationalist Party*. And this only a few months before an election was due in 1927.

The buffer zone had therefore been removed, and

British thinking was moving with increasing momentum fearing how voters from the disappearing party could now sway the issue of voting for the pro-Italian Nationalists. And their pre-occupation gained importance by the fact that a new and stronger Italy had become bolder and antagonistic and was already at the door laying claims to possession of Malta.

But the Maltese electorate seems to have given them another chance. In a closely fought election watched by all with interest and trepidation the Constitutional Party under Lord Strickland was for the first time elected with a very slight majority. So slight that there had to be recourse for help from the Labour Party under the leadership of Dr Paul Boffa whenever legislation had to be enacted. Still what concerned the British Government was that the Nationalists were in the opposition. And unable to force their italian claims.

Despite his narrow victory, Lord Strickland was boosted and supported and it soon became obvious that Britain intended taking the utmost advantage from the changed situation. Thoughts of disaster were now quickly put aside with the run of a spirit raising situation. And while worthwhile reforms were left to Strickland, the British Government could not sit back and bless the decision to strengthen the Mediterranean fleet in face of the Italian menace. In April 1929 the airfield at Hal Far was given over to the Royal Air Force, now equipped with Fairey 3 Fs and Flycatchers. Even so, however, ther were already the first pessimistic voices at the British War Offices saying that Malta could not be defended in the eventuality of a war with Italy. But that would have to be seen. If and when the situation warranted such thinking. Now it was time for consolation of the fortress which to all intents and purposes had been completed.

But it wasn't. And this was brought back with a savage jolt to the reality that had to be faced, when a purlblind Lord Strickland clashed with the Church. It seemed that the dazzling effect of all that had been achieved had momentarily diverted attention from the silent watcher that had always been the biggest power in the island.

This was the same Church that the Britis Government

had always championed. Sometimes even to the disapproval of its own protestant hierarchy. It wouldn't do to stop such backing now. On the other hand one couldn't remove Lord Strickland as this would undermine all that his party stood for. So Britain took the dispute to the Holy See. Long diplomatic discussions followed. One hotter than the other, and which were doing Britain no good with the burden of the uneasy population now being faced with challenges such as their conscience had never faced. And with another election coming.

In the meantime, Italy and the Nationalists watched from the sideline.

The climax came in 1930 with nothing substantial resulting from the discussions. The only British hope was with Strickland reconciling himself with the Church by withdrawing what damaging remarks he had made. But he didn't. So what slender hopes existed were placed with the Archbishop, then Monsignor Maurus Caruana, a cultured and erucdite Benedictine who had spent many of his earlier years at Fort Augustus Abbey in Scotland. According to Governor General Sir John du Cane, the Archbishop was favourably inclined towards the Constitutional Party, notwithstanding that the majority of his priests supported the Nationalist Party. There was also Monsignor Michael Gonzi, the same priest who had successfully contested the first election of 1921 on behalf of the Labour Party and who was now Bishop of Gozo.

But however delicate and explosive the situation might have been these dignatories of the Church had their duties and their orders to carry out. And they would not be swayed by anything or anyone else. Even in front of a powerful and influential British Government their decision was unwavering. They issued it in the form of a Pastoral Letter on 1st May, 1930. A sort of operations order to their troops who were the Maltese catholics, prohibiting their voting for Lord Strickland and his candidates in the coming election, and also those who supported him. And this under the penalty of mortal sin, and prohibition of receiving the sacraments.

Even with people having in some ways become a little more broadminded and tied up to the British kind of freedom this religious embargo was unassailable. It had been like that for centuries, and there had never appeared anything forceful enough to overpower it. The Maltese people were of course no saints. They swore, slandered, stole and swindled. They also fornicated and committed murder. But they still would not miss Sunday mass. And all the wrong and evil done, they would one day confess and repent from, to return to the fold. So they could never afford to be deprived of the Sacraments.

The British Government knew this and could foresee the outcome of the now closer election, with no pro-British horse to back. No time was lost to lodge a protest with the Holy See against what was called an ecclesiastical interference with the freedom of elections in a British Colony for the people to exercise their political judgement. But this was of no avail. The Vatican was well informed of the situation and saw no reason to change its attitude. In his final reply the Cardinal Secretary of State, who afterwards was to become Pope Pius XII, maintained that:

"The (British) Government holds that the root of the existing difficulties in Malta lies in the participation of priests in local politics. But information which had reached the Holy See and had been verified by most reliable witnesses, expressly sent thither, and especially by the Apostolic Delegate, have on the contrary made it clear that the real cause of the unsatisfactory conditions was the attitude of Lord Strickland, head of the Government, and of the Constitutional Party. An attitude undoubtedly and consistently injurious to religion, since it discredits Bishops and clergy, upsets ecclesiastical discipline and tends to destroy the religious traditions of a people so deeply attached to the Church."

Matters had reached a deadlock. The British Government could not very well contest the election with a dead horse. And it became a matter for the British Parliament to deal with. On 24th June, 1930 the British Prime Minister made a statement in the House of Commons in the course of which he said:

"In the recent Command Paper the House has been given full information regarding the intervention of the Vatican in the temporal affairs of Malta. The position which has been created by this intervention has, in the opinion of the Governor, made it undesirable for the time being to hold the General Election which is now due. In these circumstances, His Majesty's Government with considerable reluctance have decided that they have no alternative but to sanction a temporary suspension of the Constitution ... The existing Ministry will however be retained in office and will be available in a consultative capacity in so far as the Governor chooses to make use of their services."

The Constitution was thus suspended, and Malta reverted back to a Crown Colony administration. On the surface it might have appeared that Britain took the way of least resistance. But it wasn't so. There had developed a situation which favoured no side, and indeed it was the British Government which tried to restore some order in the great bland fog that surrounded it. First by pressing Lord Strickland to withdraw his offending remarks, then, when this failed, to have a Royal Commission appointed to regularize the situation. Governor du Cane too tried to prevail on Lord Strickland without success, and he too was eventually to consider him as quarrelsome. The situation was now aggravated with every attempt being made for economic development floundering in the distorted views. Both locally and in the United Kingdom also labouring under the depression which marked the thirties. When du Cane was confronted by a blank wall he resigned his governorship.

This was a bad augur for his successor Sir David G.M. Campbell. But his task was somewhat eased when the Royal Commission issued its report. The services of the Strickland Ministry should be dispensed with, it recommended, and the Constitution restored with fresh elections being held. It was certainly not the kind of recommendation Britain had hoped for. But the issue could not be avoided. There was no difficulty in dispensing with Strickland's services, but to hold elections so soon after what had happened would be too much. British preoccupation could be well understood now that there was also Mussolini's efficient propaganda machinery influencing matters. If there were to be a time to subvert any swaying this was it. But there was to be nothing to hurt Maltese feelings.

So the die was cast, and a decision taken. Malta was given back her constitution in 1932. The Royal Commission threw oil on troubled waters by expressing an opinion that any new Pastoral would now be of a different character. Strickland helped too by withdrawing his disparging remarks. An election was held soon after. But to Britain's dismay there was a Nationalist victory over the Constitutionals.

For the first time ever the much feared turmoil broke out, with the dominant element in the new government going all out to reverse the language policy. Not only of the previous ministry but also of the Imperial Government. But what seemed to be more serious was that this began to lend itself to the propagandist activities of Italian fascism, with its marching songs, its flattering uniforms, generous scholarships and other antics eloquently made up to welcome those who were considered Italy's lost children. More than just a political situation the local scene became one of hysteria, with Maltese of Italianate background finding themselves labelled as anti-British Italian fascists. If they didn't, then it was to be interpreted as treachery to the Mediterranean motherland.

It was now that Britain awoke to the nuances that had for years been inherent in the Italian language question. She had paid scant attention to them in the past. No doubt because of her ever existing complacence to Malta and her affairs. Or maybe heeding voices of those who had an interest in keeping the island in her place. It seems that now there was an examination of conscience long overdue. And while senior officials in London and Malta were suddenly being concerned with the outcome, there was the subtle strenghtening of the British fleet at Malta. The governor, Sir David Campbell, however did not mince his words when expressing his view that the parting of Britain and Malta was at hand. Indeed the question on everyone's lips was whether the island was to go to Italy, or remain as a member of the British Empire. The situation had become that serious.

A determined Britain gave the much wanted reply. It was easy to find faults in the Nationalist government's behaviour. And there were enough found to give Britain cause to suspend the Constitution again in 1933.

It was a harsh and drastic measure. Not unlike the severing of a tetanus infected limb to save the body. It was the desperate act of a Britain now no longer after her prestige. But a Britain fighting desperately to hold Malta.

CHAPTER IX

BACK ON THE ROAD TO ARMAGEDDON

The rights and wrongs of the present situation had become utterly immaterial to the issue involved. In a political sense they had gone down the drain the moment Britain found her hold on Malta to be jeopardized. All that mattered now was to dismantle what Italian influences had been built and this to be justified in the eyes of the people. Even with those too impatient to be bothered or too ignorant to understand. The biggest immediate break came for the Maltese language which was lifted from the kitchen floor to be introduced into the Courts in place of Italian. There was also a wider encouragement given for the propagation of a new style of Maltese from which Latin adulteration was expunged. Both being subtle measures to counter the Italian cutural drive, with which no Maltese could disagree. In an effort for the reapproachment to the English language there began to be offered scholarships for British universities, while the British Council was given prominence in the island. Now, more equitable conditions were offered to local servicemen, and this was marked by a steady flow of Maltese to make a career of the British Navy.

For those who could not understand there was the element of confrontation to a more aggressive Italy to be seen in the naval might which had then reached its major historical strength in Maltese harbours. The names of the majestic battleships like *Queen Elizabeth, Revenge,*

Ramillies, Repulse, Royal Oak and *Royal Sovereign* were soon on everyone's mouth. Young and old. And their presence embellished Grand Harbour. The creeks housed at least five cruisers, twenty seven destroyers and seven submarines, and the ships of this powerful armada began to be opened to visits by the public more often. Thousands of Maltese flocked to see them on Saturdays and Sundays. Admiral Sir William Fisher thought it was more fitting to give St Angelo her name back. So the name of HMS Egmont was dropped and the historical fort became HMS St Angelo again. But it was open to the public only twice a year; on the 7th and 8th September in commemoration of the Great Siege of 1565, in which it had played a very important part.

There is no doubt that this was all a part of a newly devised plan to make the officers and men of the fleet become closer to the people of Malta. And this contributed in no little way to remove some of the stigma of British arrogance which had harmed relations between the two peoples for years. What improvements were now being made in roads, the water supply system and the extension of electricity might have reflected an idea of benevolency. But they were measures which would also serve the military in the crisis that was looming ahead.

This materialized with Italy having aggressive designs on Abyssinia, and not on Malta as some were expecting. Directly Britain was not involved; however, being as it was committed to the League of Nations to prevent such a conflict she had to impose sanctions which eventually were a dismal failure. This brought Italian wrath and a convenient enough excuse to lay claim for the occupation of Malta.

It now became evident that the reconciliation Britain had sought with Malta was going to pay dividends. The fleet found ready cooperation when it was strengthened. And now there were more warships being added to become overnight the darlings of the population. The battle cruisers *Hood* and *Renown* found their berth in Grand Harbour together with the aircraft carriers *Courageous* and *Glorious*. There were added nine cruisers and a flotilla of minesweepers to increase the mighty armada to 67 ships.

The preoccupation of an inevitable conflict, however, did not register heavily in Malta because of the alternative positive effect it had on the country. In work, earnings and general economic improvements, Maltese economy was still as always dependent on war and crisis. There were also the occasions to mitigate tension. Like the silver jubilee of King George V and Queen Mary for whom Malta showed the characteristic warmth of her regard. But there were also the moments when war became so imminent that the British Government had to resort to measures like distributions of gas masks, setting up refugee camps, establishing air-raid shelters and protecting art treasures. All of them being measures received with lively interest by the public. Only the pundits saying that the British might have inflated a crisis to the dimension of a global tragedy. But behind it all there was the symbolism of the equanimity of the British Government ... which in the past might have brought disguised resentment by subversive voices. This time too it brought arguments by Army and Royal Air Force authorites that Malta was indefensible from an Italian attack. As if they would not find the smallest hope for the elaborate fortifications perfected throughout the years, the mighty navy and the trained British and Maltese troops that would have to face the onslaught if it came. But good sense prevailed and their pessimistic warning might have been instrumental in having the Royal Air Force strength at Hal Far airfield augmented by No. 23 and No. 74 Squadrons of Hawker Demon aircraft, as well as Vildebeest aircraft of both No. 22 Squadron and the Coastal Defence Development Flight. For the first time there were also sent 12 anti-aircraft guns for the island's defences.

Much as there was British interest in the awesome war preparations their ghastly purpose was very often being lost with simple Maltese humour. They were often being looked at as some new experience or pastime. When a mock air-raid was carried out on Valletta people tended to find vantage points to follow what was going on rather than take shelter. A massive display of searchlights brought the spirit of a festa, and when churchbells rang to signify the order to put all lights out, people turned out to cheer. This might have given food for thought to the sceptics that the Maltese would never adapt themselves to the conditions of any eventual war. But time was to prove otherwise.

These bizarre manouvres ended in 1936 when the crisis was over. The people now had occasion to express their sorrow for the demise of King George V. Then they gave vent to the curious in their character to follow the dynastic crisis of King Edward VIII. In the months that followed they were soon slipping back into the characteristic easy going day to day existence as life went by. Leaving what arguments were to be made to the *Times of Malta*, the new daily English paper started by Lord Strickland in 1935 and which was to play a significant part in British/Maltese relations of the future.

It wasn't the same in Britain. The Government had turned a page in the book of history of mankind. Prime Minister Stanley Baldwin retired to the House of Lords with an Earldom and was succeeded by Neville Chamberlain. He was the youngest son of the Victorian statesman who had to do so much with Malta as Colonial Secretary just before the onset of the twentieth century. The new Prime Minister took as his principal aim the bringing about of an appeasement between the Powers of Europe. Something that was considered necessary if civilisation were to be saved from annihilation which would result from another war. It was not going to be an easy task since all the nationalist passions all over the world which had led to the last great war were again at work, stirring up mankind to cruelty, wickedness and folly.

But it was not to be. The first symptom of the decadency that was to follow was the continued decline of the League of Nations. The second was the rise of Hitler. The German Leader was soon taking out Germany from the League of Nations to be followed by Japan. Italy followed their example after the organisation had tried to prevent her conquest of Abyssinia. Then like a bolt from the blue in the spring of 1936 German troops occupied the Rhineland which had been demilitarized by the Treaty of Versailles. There was worse to follow. Only a few months later a military rebellion erupted against the Spanish Republic which was planned in advance with the Fascist Government in Italy. And it was not long when Germany and Italy joined up in an 'anti-Comintern Pact' to resist, they said, the advance of Bolshevism wherever it might appear outside Russia. Italian aircraft and submarines now supporting the rebels in Spain found ample opportunities to attack British shipping "by mistake" despite promises of non-intervention. Italian troops consolidated their aggression of Abyssinia by occupying Addis Ababa, the capital. More than being appeased, the Powers of Europe had again taken the road to Armageddon.

Britain found respite in a different situation in Malta. But the biggest relief was in the knowledge that the island has passed her test as a fortress with full marks. Now with the imminence of war Britain knew that she would not do without her. But if any confirmation of the island's utility were needed it was forthcoming even in those days of troubled peace. With an acute shortage of friendly ports because of the political situation it had to be Malta to house and care for the Mediterranean fleet. There was also the Spanish rebellion now turned into a civil war which involved the British fleet in providing warships to evacuate refugees and watch over British citizens. None of the ships could afford to be too far from Malta. Hers was a service which merited the return of her constitution. But the time was now probably inopportune. With a war likely to break at any moment, and the political scars of the early thirties still evident enough to sway the issue. There were also esponiage activities by the Italian consul to be suppressed, and an Italian Culture Institute which had to be closed. These weren't isolated cases; there were people in high positions to be screened. And two of them in government employment were in fact dismissed for their pro-Italian sympathies. Much as italian influence had waned it had not yet disappeared altogether. Under those circumstances Britain could not afford to grant the constitution. Instead, there was another one given, providing for a local Executive Council, in which were roped men of all moderate political beliefs. Like Dr Paul Boffa, the leader of the Labour Party, Dr Carmelo Mifsud-Bonnici an eminent lawyer, Mr Edgar Arrigo, a businessman and Dr

P.P. Debono, a renowned surgeon. The same criteria was used for the official side of the Council, and men like Sir Philip Pullicino and Mr James Galizia served on it. The last named being later described by the Lieutenant Governor Sir Harry Luke as the best colonial treasurer he had ever met.

It was however felt to be essential that the people should know of the circumstances that had made this necessary. Also that this arrangement would still close further what breaches that might have remained. It had to be the governor to carry out this act of good faith. An apt person like Sir Charles Bonham-Carter who took office in 1936 with the particular terms of reference to bring more cordial relations between the British and Maltese. He became tireless right from the very start, paying visits to all the towns and villages of Malta and Gozo. Not the kind of formal visits one would have expected, but going all out to meet and speak to people at all levels and even to children. He made it a habit too of visiting band clubs. These were then institutions with a far wider significance than the merely musical. After the parish church the band club was the most important nucleus of the township. Within its portals there would assemble every evening a cross section of the local people. The learned and the ignorant, the well to do and the poor. And whatever problem arose to affect the inhabitants was bound to be resolved in there.

I remember Sir Charles Bonham Carter very well from that day when he visited Vittoriosa which was my home town. I was then a young boy on my first parade as a wolf cub with the local Boy Scouts troop. I remember watching him inspect our ranks, tall and lordly, with a monacle held firmly in his right eye, which he kept in place even when stooping down to talk to me. That occasion brought on me the wrath of my school mistress on the following day, who showed her disdain in no uncertain way for my having joined the Boy Scouts and taking part in that parade. She was an Italianate and was doing what she felt was her bit. I often wondered what she might have said had I joined the *Balilla*, the Italian equivalent to the Boy Scouts, which had also been introduced in Malta, although it never gained much ground.

136

Flashes like these continued to dominate the Malta scene in those days. But in the meantime Italian street names were fast changing to English, and the police began wearing British uniforms. Even telephone boxes were changed to be identical with those of London. To follow the trend there were even personal names changing version. So Giovanni became John and Giuseppe became Joe. Carmelo changed to Charles as Giovanna became Jane. Malta was returning to the fold. But for what?

There was now Hitler's occupation of Austria in 1938, which was no capricious move. And much as there were to be attempts of appeasment it became evident for all to see that the world was heading for war. Indeed there were British statesmen frankly unrealistic about the impending situation, and arguments were set forth to carry conviction that Germany would not fight Britain. But wisely enough re-armament measures were accelerated. And this too, the many false prophets said, was bound to diminish the danger of the situation.

It was the same kind of prejudice which was now again prevailing with regard to Malta, no doubt still being generated by subversive elements in the United Kingdom. The Royal Air Force was still persisting in its belief that with Sicily only thirty minutes flying time away Malta could not be defended from any Italian air attacks. And the Army too was still showing apprehension of having to beat back what Italian hordes might attack Malta from nearby Sicily. It was only the Royal Navy that resisted these views and putting arguments which seemed to have not been considered by the objectors. It was a known fact that Malta was Britain's most important base in the Mediterranean with all the latest repair facilities which were not available elsewhere. How could these be utilised if the island were to be abandoned? The First Lord of the Admiralty who had visited Malta only a year before was convinced that the island, more than Alexandria, could safeguard sea communications to the Middle East and disrupt those between Italy and North Africa.

Malta was not participating in this debate. Her people were only relying on prayers in a sincere attempt to avert war. When that year there was an Italian naval squadron

137

going on cruise to the island, and the Ali Littoria aircraft were still flying their daily mail and passenger service from Sicily they grew more hopeful that their prayers were being answered. So when the night skies continued to be scanned by searchlights in training the occasion became normal and expected. The old forts which were becoming alive after having lain dormant for years were soon attracting sightseers, and engagement in the Royal Malta Artillery and the King's Own Malta Regiment became an adventure for the young and unemployed. The first indication that things were not as good as they appeared came when 300 British wives and children were taken back to England, and reservists arrived in Malta to join the mobilising fleet. When work was hastened on Ta' Qali airfield the situation could not be ignored any longer. But while relief was being found in the powerful fleet that filled the harbour and the troops that could be seen everywhere, there was not a single aircraft to be seen in the skies. None knew that what fighting aircraft there had been were all withdrawn. Indeed, whether there would be any aircraft to defend the island was still under discussion in the British Cabinet now seemingly in a frenzy about the matter. It had to be Hore-Belisha the Minister for War to bring sense to the unending arguments.

"If we were to give up the defence of Malta," he summed up, "it would mean giving up the challenge for supremacy in the Mediterranean. But if it is decided not to defend her, then there is no point in leaving a garrison and equipment, as we already have there, just to be overrun."

Whether this had any effect or not the Cabinet reached a decision. Malta was to be defended. And in summer of 1939 the Committee for Imperial Defence laid down a defence plan based on allocating 172 anti-aircraft guns to Malta and what was more important, four fighter squadrons. A few weeks later, on 3rd September 1939, Britain declared war on Germany.

Now Malta knew she was in. For better or for worse. There was the feeling, however, that this time her role was not going to be as a logistics base, as had been the case in previous wars. But as a combattant, to knock and get knocked. Even though none could explain it this was the general feeling of the crowds that filled the streets and squares on that fateful morning of 3rd September. They always did on Sundays, chatting and laughing off worries accumulated during the week. But now they were silent, with everyone looking askance as if surprisd, maybe even thrilled, to have all been drawn into something they did not understand. As they continued to listen to the news on the radio there were only looks of puzzlement and perplexity on the sea of faces trying to follow all that was being said. As if all were fervently wanting to know too the shape of things to come.

The first shock came when they saw the fleet leaving. Battleships, aircraft carriers, cruisers and destroyers followed each other out of harbour leaving behind them many tearful eyes and throbbing hearts. Grand Harbour was soon looking so empty and futile without them. And from that moment Malta looked so vulnerable.

But this was only a symbolic thought. No one was more anxious now to get started than the Maltese. There began the daily queues of people to be issued with gas masks and those who were not otherwise engaged were soon volunteering for the Passive Defence units. A scheme was laid down to have the towns and cities around Grand Harbour and the dockyard evacuated should things come to the worst. Dockyard workers ensured a safe place in the villages for their families. But as for themselves they were given anti-aircraft guns so that if the enemy attacked they would leave their tools to take up the guns and defend their dockyard. This is how the Dockyard Defence Battery came into being. Maltese life became a routine of preparations for war, breaking down only to learn with sorrow of the loss of ships they knew so well. First there was the aircraft carrier *Courageous*, then the battleship *Royal Oak*. They mourned the lost men, particularly Maltese ratings who were lost with both ships. Then they were back to their work and the sorrow infused them with more fervour.

With the coming of 1940 they were soon following Mussolini's rantings about the mighty Regia Aeronautica and if there had been any doubt about Italy's intentions they were quickly dispelled. One comforting thought was that Britain was mobilizing the island. It was sending guns, troops and ammunition. It had even sent Air Commodore Maynard to take command of the Royal Air Force units. But as yet there had been no aircraft. This should have worried them. But faith in Britain had become stronger than fear. And with each month that went past they became more wary and less hopeful. It was only in June tht they feared the worst, when with Mussolini now showing clearly where he was jumping, the British Government had completed the three airfields in Malta, and had also an Air Officer Commanding for the last five months. But had as yet not sent one single fighter plane of the four squadrons planned a year before.

None wanted to believe it. But it appeared as if Britain had let Malta down. Was this to be the last blow of those behind the subversive voices that had plagued British/Maltese relations for more than a century?

But whatever it was there was no time for lamenting. For on 10th June, 1940 Italy declared war on Britain and Malta found herself in the front line. With a few guns, but not a single fighter plane to confront the 200 plus of Italian aircraft ready to pounce on her from their airfields, only 60 miles away.

CHAPTER X

PARTNERS IN BATTLE AND A SIEGE

The news of the Italian declaration of war on 10th June, reached Malta through the radio. No sooner had Mussolini's bombastic shouting from Palazzo Venezia in Rome died down that the word spread round like wildfire.

Malta was immediately astir. The inhabitants of the towns around Grand Harbour who had ignored government's advice to evacuate now rose in a frenzy and began to gather their belongings to take themselves to some place of security. Servicemen and policemen who happened to be at home reported for duty at once. But the streets soon emptied as everyone hurried to the nearest set of the broadcast relay service to listen to the governor who was to speak to the nation.

Lieutenant General William Dobbie had replaced Sir Charles Bonham Carter when war with Italy had seemed inevitable. He had had no delusions about his post when he took over, and knew what to expect. But like the people he governed he was a man of stubborn faith, and in difficult moments his only recourse was to the bible which he always carried with him, and to Providence it represented. This was indeed the gist of his speech that evening. With his calm and measured voice imploring divine aid to make everyone carry out his duty unflinchingly. When his speech was over the people dispersed to their homes. But there were those who thought it fit to go to Valletta where members of the Italian community were being taken for internment after being rounded up. Every vantage point along Kingsway was soon packed up and the crowd would break into patriotic shouting and the singing of the *Marseillaise* every time a group of internees was brought over. That evening what doubts about Malta must have lingered in British minds because of Italian influence were settled once and for all.

In the meantime the exodus that had started from the target area continued. Those who could not take to the villages were soon finding alternative accommodation in bastion tunnels which had been opened beforehand for such purpose. The people of Valletta and Floriana found ready-made shelter in the old disused railway tunnel joining the two towns. By the time all movement had ceased, there wasn't a soul to be seen in the streets. Malta became a silent island of darkness, as if all understood it was no time to create any problems.

The only burning problem was of British doing. It lay with Air Commodore Maynard who had been left holding three airfields without any planes. After months of pleading and requests without any tangible results there had come the time when something had to be done. It was fate or Providence that had made the aircraft carrier *Glorious* leave hurriedly for the Norwegian campaign in May. In the hurry and bustle of the moment leaving eight cases of stores on the dockside at Kalafrana. When it was found out that the cases contained Gloster Gladiator biplanes, it was easy for Maynard to get Admiral Cunningham release four of them. Their contents were rapidly assembled and rigged to give birth to four Gladiator fighters ready to take to the air. Finding the men to fly them was another desperate improvisation of Maynard since he could only count on pilots who had long been assigned clerical duties. But he did it and had his planes ready on time to form his air defence to meet any Italian onslaught. The sleepless night that followed the 10th June was wrought with fear and trepidation for Air Commodore Maynard. He was reluctant to think what the morrow would bring. And he could only find relief in the knowledge that the situation he and Malta had found themselves in, was not of his doing, and his conscience was clear. But the same could not be said for those in the United Kingdom

142

who had brought this about.

The 11th June dawned with its usual splendour. Blue skies and gold light glittering on towns and villages nestling beneath their respective cupolas and belfries. But even at that early hour of dawn there was more than the usual movement in the streets. Excitement must have made all rise earlier on that day. There were the usual throngs of workmen proceeding to work; and women chattering and gesticulating as they walked to church. In the streets of towns in the target area cars and carts were in abundance still carrying belated evacuees with their belongings. But otherwise there was nothing to show that it was not a normal day.

There was only the empty harbour, looking forlorn and helpless, to jolt one into remembrance that there was a war on. What little activity there had been on the previous day from the monitor *Terror* and the gunboats *Aphis* and *Ladybird* was now missing since the three of them had changed berth to another harbour. There was however an eddying column of black smoke rising from behind the ramparts to indicate that at least there was one ship which was alive that morning. It was indeed *HMS Fermoy*, an old coal burning minesweeper that was making steam in preparation for her daily sweep of the Maltese channel.

The only other unusual activity was in the dockyard. Not in the docks, the jetties or workshops. But on the bastions, where men of the Dockyard Defence Battery clad in their clean blue overalls were polishing their guns. Not because they needed it, but more in the way as a child fondles a new toy. Had one been able to see inside the forts and anti-aircraft batteries spread out all over the island he would have been able to detect the men of the Royal Malta Artillery now stripped to the waist after an early reveille seeing to last things before the impending battle. Determined and purposeful. Maybe even a little excited. Why not? After all, so much depended on the outcome of the test they were being put to. Not only to Malta but also to Britain. And as they carried on there were all the Maltese people behind them. Hoping and praying God that they would not fail in this which was to be their first test. And there must have been similar hopes in British hearts who might have been following those tense moments. Albeit spiced with a little uncertainty.

For another hour that seemed much longer everything continued normally. Then at ten minutes to seven there were the sirens wailing for the much expected air-raid warning.

Pandemonium broke loose. People caught in the streets were running and shouting as if the world had come to an end. Those who happened to be close to an air-raid shelter scrambled to it. Others who weren't didn't bother. They just ran to the first cover, whether this was a shop, house or church. Then all the noise dissolved as if at the wave of a magic wand, and silence reigned supreme everywhere.

Radar had in the meantime given a plot of ten plus. Detectors at the forts indicated a northerly direction, and the gunners were soon scanning the skies with their bare eyes itching to go into action. They could soon hear the deep sound of engines and spotters were now scanning the blue skies with their binoculars. Then an excited shout went out as they saw them. Ten planes with the sun glittering on their aluminium bodies. A formation of seven followed by a small one of three flying at some 20,000 feet. Above them there were the glistening dots that were the escorting fighters.

The sunburnt men on the guns watched the aircraft approach the coast, curbing with difficulty their growing excitement. Minutes flew that looked like hours. Then at last came the order to open fire. The gunners took only a second or two to make the sign of the cross. Then they blazed away. In between sounds of gunfire there floated from gun positions the sound of singing. Indeed some gunners were singing the "God Save the King". But to outdo what has by then become a poetic symphony there was soon the whining of falling bombs with the explosions that followed jerking ground and buildings in shudderin waves of shock. British seamen from *HMS Terror* and the other gunboats joined in the melee with their guns. Even *HMS Fermoy* opened up with her old 12 pounder but had to stop when shells began to drop back unexploded.

If there was some sort of order amongst the defenders in this that was their first action something different was happening with the civilian population. In houses and

144

cellars where people had taken shelter there was weeping and hysteria, particularly in the areas under bombardment. Often mufflied by sound of explosions, falling masonry and the barking guns. But not in churches where most of the people had taken shelter. The fear in there was evident only in the looks on the hundreds of faces and the movement of unrest as all were glancing at the roof and pillars holding the arches as if to assess whether they would hold if the church was hit. In there voices were not raised in crying or screaming, but in prayer, which rose in crescondo with every explosion that was heard from outside. Then suddenly all noises stopped. There was no more gunfire and no more falling bombs. Hearts throbbed with expectation. And in the silence that followed there was heard a new sound of aircraft engines that somehow came sweet to the ear, to be followed soon after with another of intermittent machine-gun fire. The people knew what it was, and fresh prayers began to rise from relieved hearts, this time for the British pilots. Many however could not resist any longer and rushed outside. Ignoring dangers and regulations to be able to shake their fists and shout damnation at the Italian aircraft now flying out of formation and chased by the Gladiators which Maynard had scrambled.

This was the first attack on Malta. Bringing initial destruction as well as the first casualties. Six more followed until sunset. But the tally for the day was closed with a heavier attack. This time by twenty five bombers in formation of five converging from all directions, dropping bombs on the way but all intent to press their attack on the dockyard. For the first time the part-timers of the Dockyard Defence Battery went into action with great zest that made them look like experienced full-timers. But damage and casualities were this time higher.

All in all people and defenders had come out of their first confrontation with the enemy with flying colours. What the guns could not do because of the enemy's flying out of range was left to the Gladiators. They started with being four, but one of them was so badly damaged after the day's fighting that Air Commodore Maynard knew he would henceforth have to rely on three. But how long would these last?

Indeed this was the question on every Maltese mouth during the first moments of respite which lent to sober meditation. It became evident from the amount of ammunition used on that first day that what remained could not last for ever. Having resisted that first day's onslaught did not delude anybody in thinking that Italian intentions had been thwarted. There were bound to be more relentless attacks which would eventually make the island ripe for an invasion which there was no hope to resist with the five infantry battalions Britain had stationed there. To the many questions that were arising everyone was looking at Britain for the answers, where the plight of Malta was being watched. What nobody knew was how much it was being appreciated. But there were certainly no rush decisions being taken in Britain, and in the days that followed Malta continued to be hammered, with her people settling down to contain the attacks and the gunners getting bolder and more accurate with their guns. But the symbol of the island's growing resistance lay in the three Gladiators now adaptly christened *Faith, Hope* and *Charity*, these being the three virtues on which the catholic faith is based. A good comparison with the three elements of the aerial defence which drove home the tensity of the situation. When at least there was a reaction from Britain this was in the form of a query from a department of the Admiralty in London asking why Fleet Air Arm property had been turned over to the RAF.

Two weeks later the orginator of that query must have been struck dumb when France surrendered. The western half of the Mediterranean was now laid wide open necessitating coverage by an already extended British fleet based at Alexandria. Now there was Winston Churchill to realise the danger of the Malta situation and to shake up friend and foe in the Cabinet to have the island held at all costs. Fighters were to be sent to beleagured Malta, as well as food supplies, more guns, troops and ammunition. His encouraging directions were reflected in Malta where Air Commodore Maynard badly pressed in his air defence desparately resorted to another stratagem to obtain two Hurricane fighters originally intended for the Middle East which helped in no little way to keep the Italians at bay. By 23rd July the number of Italian air raids had reached 80, but the general outlook was now a positive one. Rather than lamenting their destroyed buildings and mourning their dead the Maltese were busily feeling big in having resisted a much stronger enemy. And to emphasise the outcome there was the tally of twelve Italian planes shot down by the defences with the loss of only one British fighter.

What was more important was that now a no longer complacent Britain was showing recognition of meritorious services in Malta in the way of decorations which began to be awarded to members of the three services that had withstood the Italian onslaught. Men from the Royal Air Force, the Royal Malta Artillery, and the civilian population which in this case could indeed be considered as the third services. There was a change for the better, now being clearly reflected in the behaviour of the people which seemed to infuse them with more will and determination. But the climax came on 2nd August when Churchill's orders began to materialise and twelve Hurricane fighters were flown to Malta from the aircraft carrier *Argus*. More than reinforcing the depleted island's defences this had the significant meaning that the British belief of Malta being untenable had disappeared. Soon after, it was the turn of Admiral Sir Andrew Cunningham to return to the island with an array of naval might escorting a number of merchant ships laden with provisions. Even while Admiral Somerville left Gibraltar for Malta with a similar force carrying munitions, guns and more troops.

Lord Strickland died in August 1940, and his daughter, Miss Mabel Strickland, took over the running of Progress Press with its three newspapers which were to play an important part in the dramatic times there were to follow.

By the end of September Italian attacks had dwindled in numbers, frequency and intensity, and there was a change of tide. The people themselves were quick to realise this was the time to try and return to normality as far as possible. Many evacuees began going back to their homes, schools became regular and shops reopened for business.

147

The local authorities availed themselves of the situation to increase shelter accommodation, this time resorting to digging in rock. As always quick to take a hint, private families began to dig their own private shelters in ditches which soon gave rise to small communities. But all this belonged to Malta and her people. For Britain there was the fortress which had not yet been exploited. Now was the time to do it.

Notwithstanding his initial victories over the Italian army in North Africa General Wavell had still to contend with an enemy which was still superior in numbers. But the biggest handicap lay in that the Italians could still transport troops and equipment at will and maintain a fluid situation. Nothing had as yet been attempted to stop this regular reinforcement at will and only 2 per cent was sunk of the 700,000 tons of shipping that had plied between Italy and North Africa. It was then obvious that Malta could fill this breach. Particularly at this time when Britain could send very little help to Wavell who was often handicapped by reinforcements failing to reach him from Egypt. It was now too that Churchill was chasing a different hare in thinking of sending British units to Greece which would weaken still further Wavell's forces.

In November, Royal Air Force units in Malta were strengthened with Swordfish torpedo bombers, and a squadron (No. 37) of Wellington bombers. Submarines of the Mediterranean fleet were now diverted to Malta for their replenishments and refits which placed them in a better position to attack Italian shipping. Even the bigger elements of the fleet were now availing themselves of Malta's breathing respite to call at Grand Harbour in the process of trying to find and engage the Italian fleet and this also marked the re-ascendancy of the British fleet in the Mediterranean. As if to confirm this on 11th November the Fleet Air Arm attacked Taranto harbour at night and sank the pride of the Italian navy, the battleship *Cavour* and seriously damaged two other capital ships the *Littorio* and *Caio Diulio*.

There is no doubt that the offensive activity from Malta had a marked effect on the enemy. Directly by sinking 109,089 tons of shipping in 4 months, and indirectly by forcing Italian forces to fall further back in North Africa pressed as they were by the lack of equipment, and provisions which failed to reach them. This turned into a disaster with the loss of not less than 130,000 men in prisoners for only 2,000 British casualties including the wounded. It was also badly timed for the Axis, coming as it did when Hitler was having plans for the Eastern Mediterranean which he could not carry out if North Africa was lost to him. So being now convinced of Italian incapability to hold the British forces he forced German assistance for North Africa on Mussolini. This was to be in the form of German troops and Panzers. But first he had to ensure a clear passage from Italy to North Africa, and this could be done by first ordering the Luftwaffe to subdue the base of Malta.

Fliegerkorps X was moved to Sicily in December 1940. But one of its first impressive actions was to intercept one of the biggest British naval forces which was escorting two convoys from East and West under the respective admirals Cunningham and Sommerville, one of which was heading for Malta. It was obvious that the Luftwaffe would press home its attack on the Malta convoy under Admiral Cunningham in his flagship *Warspite*. With him he had two other battleships, the *Valiant* and *Barham* as well as the aircraft carriers *Eagle* and *Illustrious* besides seven cruisers and sixteen destroyers. The attack came when the convoy was some 80 miles away from Malta but the German planes unleashed their fury on the *Illustrious* which was severely hit and crippled. From then onwards it became a running battle for the aircraft carrier as it continued limping with the convoy until it reached Malta during the night. Dawn transformed the ship into a forest of torn and twisted steel soon to be surrounded by surveyors and workmen assigned the impossible task to make the ship seaworthy. Until this could be done she had to lie there, alongside a wharf in the dockyard like a sitting duck. It was there that the Luftwaffe found her on 16th January, 1941. Forty four Stukas Junkers 87, seventeen Junkers 88, ten Messerschmitt 110, ten Italian Fiat CR42 fighters and a number of Macchi 200. But now the *Illustrious* was not alone. As the combined German and Italian force reached Grand Harbour it seemed as if hell was let loose. The batteries round the harbour opened rapid fire to be joined by every warship that was in port. The sky bcame like a blazing inferno. Yet the Germans carried on with the Stukas diving through walls of burning steel to drop their bombs on the target which was the aircraft carrier. The Dockyard Defence Battery and other light guns that had been added to the defence of the harbour met them with their Bofors and Pom-Poms, but the Germans didn't falter. The harbour became a cauldron of smoke and water spouts from exploding bombs, and made more sinister by the din of the murderous gunfire. When the barrage fell silent it was to let in the Hurricanes, the Fulmars and the remaining two Gladiators to join in the scuffle. But even before these could return to their base after the raiders had left there was a second wave to repeat the performance.

When the attack was over the dockyard was like a sea of craters and ruined sheds. What had been an arsenal of activity now stood out as a stark macabre picture. The towns around the dockyard, all patrimonies of the Knights, had also been badly hit. Churches, auberges and whole blocks of building were all razed to the ground. Nothing seemed to move in that desolation except the fires that were still burning and the eddying dust. But as this cleared *Illustrious* emerged like a phantom. Hit again, but still afloat.

The Germans attacked again on the 18th January, this time their target being the airfields. There were more than 200 enemy aircraft involved and the defences again rose as one. Then attacks were again pressed home on the 19th, this time back to the harbour and the *Illustrious*, laying more havoc to buildings, but not succeeding in sinking their target ship. The Germans lost 39 aircraft in those three attacks, with another 14 probables. But this was a small recompense for the damage and devastation they caused. Day and night, Maltese workmen worked on the aircraft carrier racing against time to patch her up before the Germans would return. On 24th January, 1941 the work was completed and the *Illustrious* sailed away that same night for Alexandria to fight another day.

German attacks were renewed with vigour on 2nd

February. This time they were mainly directed against the airfields. At the same time General Wavell was wiping out the last of Italian resistance in North Africa taking 20,000 prisoners, 216 guns and 120 tanks. On 6th February Hitler summoned General Erwin Rommel and ordered him to go to North Africa and take over two divisions, the 15th Light and 15th Panzer. So the Luftwaffe intensified its attacks on Malta to keep British offensive aircraft grounded while German forces were crossing over. German persistence was impeccable, destroying aircraft and installations. But so were the defences, shooting them down. Day after day, and week after week life in Malta became like a routine of air battles and whining bombs, destruction, and casualties. Fortunately enough there were by now enough rock shelters for everybody. But there was nothing to prevent the mass devastation of buildings.

It was strange how the people who had ran away in panic in the first Italian raids which were already being considered to have been a joke when compared to the German assault, were now surmounting all fears and pre-occupations and continuously trying to resume normal living. They went underground to escape the bombs, but when raids were over they would come out to continue where they had left. Or even to start afresh. To give them heart there was the Governor General William Dobbie, who in the worst days during this month of February was telling them on the radio how the three services and the civilian population were all four square in their fight. There was also Winston Churchill paying tribute to the Maltese defenders and the Dockyard workers. "The eyes of all Britain and indeed the whole British Empire are watching Malta in her struggle day by day," he had said, "and we are sure that success as well as glory will crown your efforts."

One person, however, who might not have been appreciative of the situation in Malta was strangely enough the First Sea Lord Admiral Sir Dudley Pound. When pressed by Admiral Cunningham to provide transport for more Hurricanes to be sent to Malta he was adamant to risk more aircraft carriers after what had happened to *Illustrious* and emphasized priority to be given to the

Battle of the Atlantic, which, in his opinion, transcended all other things. His, must have sounded like another of the subversive voices of some years back. It was because of this stand that 21 Hurricanes were loaded on a cargo steamer *Parracombe* with ground staff and equipment, and made to sail independently from Gibraltar. Only to be lost on the way.

But more than all the praise that was forthcoming there was the Royal Navy to raise spirits all round. Even in this time of woe with the island literally fighting for her existence there was a convoy of four ships brought safely to harbour after eluding only God knows what dangers. It was indeed followed by German aircraft right to harbour and the defences combined to protect it. Hurricanes, and anti-aircraft gunners brought down 13 of the raiders. There were also now four destroyers stationed in Malta, the *Jarvis*, *Janus*, *Nubian* and *Mohawk* and a small flotilla of 'U' class submarines: *Upright*, *Utmost*, *Unique*, *Urge*, *Ursula*, *Upholder*, *Union* and *Usk*. Together forming a combined force striking at Italian shipping carrying stores and equipment to Rommel in North Africa. The Royal Air Force too rose again now with its bombing raids on Sicily and Italy, and its torpedo bombers going for enemy shipping that could not be reached by the navy. As if to cap the air of optimism that became evident in those days the navy managed to engage the Italian navy at Cape Matapan and scored a resounding victory.

It had by now become evident that nothing less than an invasion would stop Malta from being a thorn in the enemy's side. Indeed there had already been German thoughts about it, but Hitler now had other plans on his mind. There were Greece and Yugoslavia attacked and occupied on 6th April. Then on the 20th there was the invasion of Crete from the air, which drove home the imminence of a similar attack on Malta. With the arrival of more Hurricanes the RAF defences were re-organised, and the Command expanded. Air Vice Marshal Maynard was replaced by Air Vice Marshal Hugh P. Lloyd.

The closest the enemy came to the feared invasion was in July 1941 when the Italian *Decima Flottiglia Mas* attempted to enter Grand Harbour to sink a convoy that had just arrived. This ensemble under its *commandante* Valerio J. Borghese was equipped with human torpedoes and *barchini* which were small boats carrying an explosive charge leaving only enough space for its motor and the pilot with an ejector seat which he could dislodge to shoot himself away before the moment of contact and explosion. There were eleven of these boats participating in the attack on Malta carried in the tender *Diana*, together with a Human Torpedo Launcher carrying the human torpedoes and their crews, all under Commander Moccagatta. Accompanying them there were also two MAS boats to pick up the ejected crews. What the attackers did not know was that when they left Augusta in Sicily at midnight they were already detected by the Malta radar, and the coast defence was alerted. When they reached the Maltese coast just before dawn, one of the participants, Maggiore del Genio Teseo Tesei proceeded right up the breakwater's side viaduct with his human torpedo while the rest of the flottiglia stayed put some two miles away. The plan was for him to blow up his torpedo and break down the anti-submarine net in the entrance when the boats would be able to rush into the harbour. Teseo Tesei carried out his suicidal assignment, but at his explosion the sea outside Grand Harbour was illuminated by searchlights and the Maltese gunners of the coast defence went into action with their multiple six-pounders. Even anti-aircraft gunners turned their Bofors seawards and joined in the melee. The explosion had in the meantime brought down the span of the viaduct which blocked the entrance Teseo Tesei had opened up. There was still no time to think of this since the Italian boats were being blown to blazes in a question of minutes. Four of them which tried to run away were sunk by Hurricanes which had been scrambled to intercept the Italian fighters that had accompanied the attackers, none of which returned to base.

The rest of 1941 continued unchanged as far as air attacks were concerned. But the submarine offensive from Malta had gathered momentum and between June and September sank eleven enemy supply ships totalling about 75,000 tons. 16 others totalling 41,000 tons were sunk by submarines from Gibraltar and Alexandria raising the total to 116,000 tons which represented 50% of what was being sent to Rommel. Wellingtons and Blenheims continued to hammer Sicilian bases and Hitler was soon complaining to Mussolini about the lack of protection that was being given to reinforcements to North Africa. The effect was being reflected there with Rommel having to go on the retreat. It was this that made the Germans move U Boats to the Mediterranean, and when ships' losses reached the figure of 80% Hitler reacted by appointing Field Marshal Kesselring as Commander in Chief South and giving him the specific instructions to neutralize Malta once and for all.

But by now there was another danger looming ahead. Convoys had kept coming, losing ships on the way, but always managing to get some safely in port. However, the increased activities had demanded more fuel and ammunition which required heavier and earlier replenishments. Food had become short and nothing of the tinned stuff that was available would substitute the staple diet of bread and olive oil with which the Maltese were blessed. And both these items were now becoming short. A shuttle service by three submarines for delivery of food and essential supplies was re-started. But they could never carry enough. Notwithstanding a convoy having reached Malta in September, there was now the immediate need of another one being felt. If it did not, then the future of Malta would be in jeopardy. As a reminder of the difficult situation there was the aircraft carrier *Ark Royal* delivering another consignment of badly needed Hurricanes. But on its return to Gibraltar it was sunk by a German U Boat.

Field Marshal Kesselring lost no time in resuming his offensive against the island and the battle was resumed in earnest. With German aircraft from Crete already harassing convoys from Alexandria, he now intensified air operations from Sardinia to harass anything coming from Gibraltar. His airmen delivered 175 air attacks on Malta during December 1941. But the tally for January 1942 was 263. Much as he was determined to eliminate the island by bombing, and was also thinking seriously of the postponed invasion, he was nonetheless screwing up a blockade. And its effect was being felt.

There was a lot to generate hope in continued resistance and men like Sir Edward Jackson, the Lieutenant Governor, Professor A.V. Bernard, the Chief Government Medical Officer, Dr Paul Boffa, another stalwart, Lieutenant Colonel Edgar Salomone of the Royal Malta Artillery and many others were being decorated in recognition of services rendered. There were also the women, amongst whom there was Miss Mabel Strickland the new owner of and editor of the Times of Malta, which had never missed an issue. Even when the paper store was hit by bombs, the newspaper was issued with charred pages. But there was nothing to hide the once beautiful harbour that had now become a foul lake of wrecks, the dockyard that was only a rubble of cordite grey stone and the beacons from burning aircraft in the airfields that had become an every day occurance. The people had indeed disciplined themselves to endure shortages and were bearing hunger in silence, but this did not stop the dwindling of stores. Now they could fast, and the troops be placed on sleeping parades, while there was still the little to go on. But the time was getting closer when there would be none to lay hands on. Then what?

While this silent reasoning was going on there was the welcome news of a convoy being attempted from Alexandria. It was the first one since September 1941, consisting of three ships with a heavy escort. Its importance, however, must have been similarly realised by the Germans who attacked it incessantly and sank all the three ships.

It had become unbelievable how one could exist at all. And this feeling was on both sides. The British in Malta tried to bolster efforts by thinking of getting Spitfires to replace the Hurricanes which were showing their shortcomings againt the new Messerschmitts. Kesselring planned the mortal blow − a two pronged effort with first a big air assault which was to be followed by an invasion for which he had received Hitler's approval.

Worry and preoccupation had been weighing most heavily with the Governor, Sir William Dobbie. By now, he had been knighted. The eyes beneath his bushy eyebrows that many had called "magnetic" were now feverish and red as if he was not sleeping enough. His tall figure seemed that of an older man. He had suffered and borne everything with his people, and also with the same faith he had as well trusted in Divine Providence. But now he was feeling there was no escape. Rather than diminishing rations will further, which were already at a minimum, a communal feeding scheme was worked out whereby all remaining foodstuffs were pooled and cooked to provide one hot plate a day to every person. They were called Victory Kitchens, but the truth was more like a fair distribution of what was left, so that if the people were to die of hunger then they would die together.

On the 7th March, 1942 arrived the first Spitfires. Fifteen of them which had flown from the aircraft carrier *Eagle* lying south of Majorca. They went into action two days later bringing the desired hope in aerial combat. It was intended to have them followed by others from the West to coincide with a badly needed convoy of supplies from the East. Both convoys were fitted up and left for Malta on 20th March. On that same day Kesserling gave the order for the final assault to be launched on the island.

This was no mean threat. It began with German formations of 200 planes and over attacking first the airfields and other installations. Dropping a variety of bombs all tailored for the target. Including mines which wrought widespread devastation. The convoy from the West did not take long to reach a spot from where Spitfires could be launched. They flew off from *Eagle* and *Argus*, and they had hardly reached Malta when they had to be serviced and armed to scramble to fight. The other convoy, however, was not finding things so easy. It had first to fight off an Italian naval squadron which attacked it on the way. There were attacks from the Luftwaffe which turned the three day crossing to Malta into a continuously running battle. Of the four ships in the convoy one was sunk when only fifty miles away from the island. Then when the rest were only eight miles away, the second ship, *Breconshire*, was hit but fortunately it did not sink. It was towed with difficulty into the port of Marsaxlokk where the Germans continued to attack it. From then onwards it became a battle between stevedores trying to save what they could from the merchandise, and the Germans trying to prevent them. There was a closer fight with the other two ships which entered Grand Harbour.Safe and sound for only a brief moment. In the next attack both of them were hit. One of them, the *Talabot*, was set on fire and stevedores and troops began to unload before the fire reached the hold where ammunition was carried. The other ship, the *Pampas*, began sinking slowly, and here too hurried unloading was carried out sometimes with stevedores and soldiers having to jump in flooded holds to retrieve stores. It was touch and go, and 4,952 tons of stores were unloaded before both ships were lost. One of them having to be scuttled because of the exploding ammunition.

The assault continued right into April without respite and it seemed certain that Malta must fall. With Egypt now under threat of an advancing Rommel, once Maltese interception of his supplies had almost ceased, the British Cabinet was in a dilemma whether to save Malta or Egypt. It couldn't do both. And here there was no hesitation. Malta was to be saved at the risk of losing Egypt. General Auckinleck was ordered to attempt to occupy airfields in West Cyrenaica while a crash plan had to be worked out to replenish Spitfires in Malta since there were no aircraft carriers to do it at the time. There was also impressed on the Cabinet the essential change of the governor Sir William Dobbie if Malta and the Mediterranean were to be saved for the Western world. The time was fixed for Auckinleck's offensive, while the American aircraft carrier *Wasp* was borrowed to carry 47 Spitfires to the island. On 15th April, 1942 British appreciation of what Malta was doing was sealed with the award of the George Cross by King George VI.

To honour her brave people I award the George Cross to the island fortress of Malta, to bear witness to a heroism and devotion that will long be famous in history.

This was the King's message to Malta which helped in no small way to intensify resistance. In six weeks of the assault the Germans had rained 6,557,231 kilograms of bombs which was almost as much as had been dropped on the whole of Britain during the peak of her battle in September 1940. For long periods without water and electricity the Maltese people waited and hoped, while the fast minelayer *Welshman* loaded with supplies hurried on her own to break the blockade. General Lord Gort VC arrived unobtrusively to take over from Sir William Dobbie during an air-raid. And on the morrow *Eagle* delivered 61 Spitfires. The merciless pounding continued for three more days, during which the German and Italian air forces lost more planes than in the previous five weeks. The Germans had flown 11,500 sorties against the island. This was the turning point of the battle, and Kesselring reported to Hitler that his first mission was completed and the base at Malta had been eliminated.

But Malta was far from being finished. *Eagle* was soon back with 55 more Spitfires and Gort was soon getting things ship-shape again. The air-raids continued but now there again were the Spitfires, and with the ground defences destroyed 116 enemy planes during May.

The only remaining dire problem was that of supplies and two convoys set out from East and West in an attempt to remedy the situation. The one from the East, however, was so heavily attacked by the Germans from Crete that it never reached Malta. That from the West had similar difficulties but managed to bring two merchantmen and the *Welshman* safely on 16th June. What they brought was a drop in the ocean, the more so when considering the fuel and ammunition that was now required because of the impending German invasion – Operation Hercules, which was scheduled for 10 July.

Fortunately enough Rommel was then poised for his final assault on Tobruk which would open for him the way to Egypt. He badly needed Stukas for his attack which he borrowed from Kesselring. But when he did occupy Tobruk, and Kesselring asked for his aircraft back, Rommel had already taken the road of no return with an attack on Sidi Barrani. So the Stukas remained in North Africa, and Kesselring had no dive bombers to back the two parachute divisions, and the three Italian assault divisions he had prepared for the invasion. When his divergence of opinion with Rommel was referred to Hitler and Mussolini both of them had turned against it. Hitler because of the heavy losses incurred in Crete which still burned in his mind and Mussolini because the occupation of Egypt was more likely to appease his vanity. He had already sent his white charger which he wanted to ride for his entry in Cairo. So Operation Hercules fizzled out.

Air attacks continued, and there were 188 during July. But now with something like 100 Spitfires on the island under Air Vice Marshal Keith Park who had replaced Lloyd, the air situation was controlled. There came the time, however, when many of the machines had to refrain from sorties because of lack of petrol, while guns too had to remain silent because of shortage in ammunition. But the mostly felt shortage was that of food, and now the population was told of the situation. Unless there was an immediate convoy to bring enough supplies in food and fuel Malta would fall. The word went round that after all not even Gort could save Malta. It had only to be a miracle. And as they had always done the people resorted to prayer, this time with particular emphasis to Santa Maria (Saint Mary) whose feast would fall on 15th August. None of them knew of Gort's pleadings and Britain's understanding in mounting the biggest convoy which left without fuss on 10th August.

The convoy suffered its first setback when the Germans learned about it immediately it left. They had all the time to make preparations and every available aircraft and warship they could lay their hands on was thrown against it. From Sardinia to the Malta Channel the convoy was under attack by submarines, aircraft and even torpedo boats. Notwithstanding the brave fight put by crews both the ships in the convoy, 14 in all, and the warships in the escort suffered heavy losses. Nine of the fourteen ships were sank, leaving only five to limp the last few miles to the island. Amongst them these there was the tanker *Ohio* which was carrying 11,000 tons of oil fuel, making it the most important ship of them all. Without it Malta would still fall. And this was what made the Germans concentrate their last attacks on it. But the *Ohio* continued to make way after receiving six direct bomb hits. It also survived a torpedo, and an aircraft which crashed on its deck. It appeared to all that there was some supernatural force keeping the ship afloat. On the 13th August the four surviving merchantmen reached Malta. Battered, and unrecognisable through their black twisted metal, but with their cargo intact. They were taken in hand by tugs with crews all ready to fight for them to the last man, while every anti-aircraft gun on the island was on the alert, with Spitfires flying above in a continuous patrol. The population welcomed the four ships from the bastions, but there was a sad note ending their tumultous cheering after the fourth ship entered harbour, and there was no more. They all knew that without a tanker all that the island had gone through would be futile, because it could not go on.

This sense of doom continued through the next day even while the four merchantmen were being unloaded. Gort knew that the *Ohio* was somehow still afloat, but it was some two hundred miles away and in big trouble. With smashed steering gear, decks awash and still burning fires, it was cradled by two cables held fast on port and starboard by two destroyers.. It was still plodding on. But both its skipper Captain Mason and Gort in Malta were thinking the same. That only a miracle could make the ship reach Malta.

And the people's prayers were still further raised in unison to Santa Maria.

Then in the morning of the 15th while all the people were attending what makeshift church services they had, there was the word passed round that the *Ohio* had reached Malta. They all flocked to the bastions not believing their ears. But they were just in time to see the tanker being carried in port. They knew that the miracle they had prayed for had happened and Malta was saved. That epic went down in Maltese history as the story of the Santa Maria Convoy.

CHAPTER XI

SURVIVAL AND RESURGENCE

It was by no means over. Siege, battle and war were still on. The Santa Maria Convoy had only relieved the situation. After the sorrow, hardship and suffering that had been gone through the past months a respite was in sight. The Rome correspondent of the *Tribune de Geneve* carried a report that the Axis Command knowing that the last convoy had provided Malta with the required stores, had decided that for the time being there would be no further attempts of neutralizing the island. Instead, air forces would concentrate on protecting convoys to North Africa.

They could not know that after all there was still a problem with wheat. Only Lord Gort knew how he had miscalculated the amount of this commodity that had arrived with the convoy. Apparently ignoring the fact that the two ships which had carried most of their cargo in wheat had both been sunk, when he had increaed the bread ration. This could no longer be maintained, and what wheat there was, which was the main staple item of the Maltese diet, would last for less than a month with no likely convoy to be available by then. Gort was worried. And because he was worried he decided to confide his preoccupation in Monsignor Gonzi. He did not know why he had been drawn to this diminutive man to confide in him what he would not do with anyone else. And this notwithstanding what he had been told about him. Monsignor Gonzi was then still bishop of Gozo, but he was often in Malta helping the local ailing bishop Monsignor Maurus Caruana. They were the same two bishops who had in 1930 ignored British pressure and issued the Pastoral prohibiting voting for Lord Strickland under the penalty of mortal sin. They had never been forgiven. While Monsignor Caruana was past being penalized, Monsignor Gonzi was still under a British veto preventing him from ever becoming bishop of Malta. Sir Harry Luke, the Lieutenant Governor at the time had passed the word that he was anti-British, and this had stuck. But Gort found nothing to substantiate it. When he told the bishop about the critical wheat situation he got the reply he had never expected.

"I could find a remedy for you," said the bishop. "In fact I am sure I can get you all the wheat you want."

Gort could only look at him in amazement.

"How?" he said unbelievingly.

"From Gozo. It is now the time of the harvest, and if I know the Gozitans they will have enough wheat with which they will not part for anyone or anything. But for me they will do it."

There were now no more doubts with Gort.

"All right then. Will you do it Monsignor?" he said.

"Yes. But I must be permitted to divulge the state of the situation to the Gozitans, and then I must be given transport to have the wheat collected."

"Agreed," said an enthusiastic Gort.

And that was that. Monsignor Gonzi was true to his word. It only needed a circular letter over his signature to be read in Gozitan churches on the following Sunday. As he said his flock obliged and Malta had enough wheat to last her till the next convoy. And Gort knew he had been right all the time about the bishop who had laboured for twelve years under a stigma put on him by the British Government, which he did not merit.

Another British shortcoming lay with the lowly paid workers. Both at the dockyard and elsewhere. These were the same men who were being continuously praised for their stalwart collaboration under bombardment. And what recompense these people might have expected had never gone beyond this. Indeed the new sense of camaraderie that had sprung up with the British, with whom these workers were working and fighting shoulder to shoulder might have kindled what embers of servilism had existed into fires. And this must have prevented what individual attempts were occasionally forthcoming to ask for one's rights. The feeling to unite had long been growing, but it had always been postponed because of the situation, and also because there had not yet been found the man who could unite the people. Now the time seemed to be ripe, and what was more important there came forward the man who could do it.

Reggie Miller was a senior Admiralty clerk. He was the secretary to the Malta Admiralty Branch of the Civil Service Clerical Association. With this being a British trade union Miller had had to combat British autocracy several times. Moreover he was by nature a hardened campaigner. It was whilst addressing a meeting of the sections of his union that the need to unite all workers occurred to him.

"If we who represent only the clerical employees are achieving so much by uniting our efforts," he said during that meeting, "one can visualize how much more can be achieved if all the industrial workers were to be so united into one and the same union."

And his words drove the message in, which was to be an important landmark of trade unionism in Malta. Now in the lull of September 1942 he addressed a mass meeting for all workers, and his suggestion for the formation of a trade union was received by acclamation. He would no doubt have gone forward with it from there had it not been for the October blitz that followed. This began on the night of 10 October and continued without respite. Now the Air Officer Commanding, Air Vice Marshal Keith Park could put into operation his new plan of action of meeting the raiders on the way before they reached Malta. With the respectable number of aircraft at his disposal he could do it. Until 19th October when the raids stopped altogether. The Germans had flown 1400 sorties in those 10 days, losing at least 114 planes against 25 Spitfires. Those were to be the last of the German attacks on Malta. 1600 in all, which had cost them 1069 in shot down aircraft.

Even if the endeavours for the formation of a workers trade union continued there was nothing brought to the surface since it became evident to all that while one battle had ended, there was another one still to be fought. And as British aircraft were now flying daily out of Luqa, and the sleek grey submarines became more active hearts were overflowing with expectations. It became obvious that something was in the offing, and war was still taking priority over anything else, however personal.

Then finally it came, on 23rd October when Montgomery launched his offensive from El Alamein. There was nothing important enough to stop anyone following the British advance through the news. And it was only edged aside on 8th November with the Allied landings in French North Africa. The Maltese rejoiced. Because now British successes more than ever before, were also their own. Also because they realised, as indeed all the world did, that this was the turning point of the war in the Mediterranean, and Malta could now breathe freely.

Their rejoicing was such that it even dispelled all worries about the fact that on that day there only remained 25 days supplies of foodstuffs, ammunition and aviation spirit. Or maybe all were convinced Britain would not fail to despatch a convoy in time. Indeed she did. The convoy arrived on 23rd November, all intact. But what was more important, it was unmolested and this signified that the siege was lifted.

The year 1943 dawned full of hope. Maltese life began to pick up amidst the rubble of destruction. Even though the battle was not yet over. And there were some sporadic air-raids to show it. But life carried on and there were even the first repairs being taken in hand. If this were to be some sort of an interlude nobody was going to stop the people enjoying it.

The truth however was that it was only a breathing space to afford time and scope to gain strength. Not to resist or make war, but to attain what was now being imperatively felt was the island's due. Those who were responsible made sure to pass the message. But British thinking was now channelled in the same direction. As far back as 1942 the Chancellor of the Exchequer had stated in the House of

Commons that the outstanding gallantry shown by the people of Malta in the face of enemy attacks of unprecedented length and severity called for some special recognition. And notwithstanding the financial burden Britain was carrying, an immediate free gift of £10,000,000 was made there and then for the restoration of war damage and reconstruction. This not being enough, there was soon made another one of £20,000,000.

It was a much appreciated gesture, tangibly made at a time when it was most needed. But Maltese thoughts were elsewhere, and this was reflected in the speeches at a mass meeting held by Reggie Miller on 28th March which can be said to have been instrumental in giving birth to the General Workers' Union. Much as many looked on those days as teeming with hinted turbulence, facts show the contrary. Miller was harping on equivalence for Maltese workers, social services and of course a self-government. But in truth the British Government had already expressed itself to be in favour of many of the amenities that were being proposed. And his was the only voice being raised. Only that the war was far from being over, despite that the determination to win the war and win it quickly was replacing every other emotion in the people who had suffered so much.

The picture changed completely on 20th June when King George VI paid a short visit to Malta. All extraneous thoughts were put aside on that day as everyone swarmed to the bastions and vantage points around Grand Harbour to see the cruiser *Aurora* entering harbour with the white dressed figure of the sovereign who a year back had awarded them all the George Cross. The general salute fired by Fort St Angelo was drowned beneath a mightier one accorded by the church bells of the four beleagured cities surrounding the harbour. And by the mad cheering of the antlike crowds on the bastions, as well as the hundreds that filled the harbour in their colourful *dgħajsas*. And the King was moved by the tumultous welcome which was repeated every time and everywhere he went to meet the soldiers and airmen who had fought, and the men and women who had toiled and laboured under bombardment.

Maybe the only politically tinged moment of that day came when Lord Gort introduced Monsignor Gonzi.

"He has in his own time saved Malta, Your Majesty," said Gort to the King. Then he followed with the whole story of the wheat and also of British misconceptions which had unjustly stigmatized him. That visit clarified matters and the British Government was soon to remove its objections to Monsignor Gonzi's appointment as Archbishop of Malta after the death of Dom Maurus Caruana. With this appointment there was also the revival of an old custom which had died of vesting the Archbishop with the honorary rank of Major General in the British Army.

But as the King had heard and seen all of Malta there might have been his influence behind the British Government's declaration on 7th July:

His Majesty's Government have had under consideration certain representations which have been made by the elected members of the Council of Government in Malta, who have asked for an announcement regarding their intentions in relation to further constitutional development. Since the present Constitution of Malta was inaugurated in 1939 the fortress has successfully withstood a siege of two and a half years. During the siege the Island was subjected to heavy and sustained attacks from the air and to a food shortage of increasing gravity. By their steadfastness and fortitude under the severe hardships thus occasioned, the people of Malta together with its gallant garrison rendered services of incalculable value to the allied cause. . . .

For more than ten years, between 1920 and 1933, the people of Malta enjoyed full legislative and administrative responsibility under the Crown in the conduct of their national affairs, the control of naval and military services and of all matters appertaining to the position of Malta as an Imperial Fortress, or otherwise affecting imperial interests or policy, being reserved to the Imperial Government. It is the policy of His Majesty's Government that responsible government in the same sphere should again be granted to Malta

More welcome for British Royalty

(National Library of Malta)

Governor General Sir John P. Du Cane laying the foundation stone of
St. Luke's Hospital

(National Library of Malta)

Combined Army, Navy and Royal Air Force parade at Marsa, during celebrations of the Silver Jubilee of King George V and Queen Mary (National Library of Malta)

Warships of the Royal Navy of the 20th century in Grand Harbour
(The Times)

One of the many air bombardments of World War II in 1942

Damage in Valletta after one of the air raids

King George VI seeing war damage at Senglea in June, 1943
(National War Museum Association of Malta)

Princess Elizabeth (now Queen Elizabeth II) at Marsa during her stay in Malta 20/1/1949 to 28/12/1848. With her are Prince Philip with Lord and Lady Mountbatten
(National Library of Malta)

The Princess and Lady Edwina Mountbatten (National Library of Malta)

The Princess paying homage to the fallen at the Cenotaph
(National Library of Malta)

Princess Elizabeth at the Palace Ball accompanied by Governor Sir Gerald Creasy
(National Library of Malta)

Prime Minister Dr. George Borg Olivier receiving the Independence documents on 21st September, 1964
(Independence Press)

The last British governor, Sir Maurice Dorman

HMS *London* leaving Malta on 1st April, 1979

Monument at Vittoriosa commemorating the departure of British forces from Malta on 31st March, 1979 (PEG Picture Library)

HMS *Brazen* arriving at Grand Harbour on 14th August, 1986 (J. Attard)

after the war.

This declaration came at a time when Malta had again turned to the business of war and was the venue of an unprecedented concentration of troops and armour, with her harbours packed with ships and landing craft of a formidable invasion armada. What satisfaction it generated was just in time to contribute to the rousing send off to the invading armies that three days later swooped on Sicily.

Two months later, on 8th September, 1943 Italy surrendered bringing also the siege to a timely end.

* * *

In January 1944, the Maltese woke to a new kind of life. They knew that the worst was over. The streets filled up with people and there was again the familiar sound of their myriad voices in normal conversation. As if to join in the new spirit of resurrection the days were bright with sunlight, and what wintry wind there was in the blue skies swept about buildings, where they still stood, with a swift shrill cry as if to entice all for the future that seemed to dawn anew.

It was now the time for separations with men of the British garrison being posted to other theatres of operations, many of them leaving behind them wives and sweethearts; all of them leaving a host of friends. It was also time for reflection on the strong bond that had emerged between the peoples of the two nations and the price that had been paid by both parties to seal that bond. At least 15,500 buildings were destroyed, comprising 70 churches, 18 monasteries or convents, 22 schools, 8 hospitals, 5 banks and 48 of Malta's public edifices including 6 Knights' *Auberges*, all irreplacable remnants of a heritage from a past era. 1,597 civilians had been killed, 1,818 injured, some of whom maimed for life. From their end the British had lost 547 aircraft in battle in the Malta skies and the hundreds of pilots that had died with them. Another 160 aircraft were destroyed on the ground. To this there were to be added the ships that were lost in convoy in trying to carry supplies, and the crews that drowned with them. Although it was within their terms of operation there were also the many warships sunk both in and outside Maltese harbours. Amongst them two aircraft carriers whilst on their daring runs to ferry fighter aircraft. These were all facts and figures that made a balance sheet of tears from which Britain and Malta emerged closer and stronger.

Now there began to fall into place the many misforecasts that had been made about Malta. Many lessons had been learned, and as if to make up for the future there were already new projects being mentioned. Surveys were made and the ideal number of battleships and aircraft carriers for the future was being projected. All being based on the assumption that Malta will more than ever before remain Britain's impregnable base for the Mediterranean fleet.

This, however, was too premature. Because it meant that the island would have to remain for ever dependent on a military role for her existence. And Malta had learned her lessons too in this respect. Her long record of feud alism could never be forgotten. It had been like an interminable string of events to keep her shackled to that kind of history. Only that it was not yet known what to drive at.

So life was continued. The people settled back in their places and work, business continued to pick up. The farmers went back to the fields, and the masons returned to chip the white Malta stone in the blazing sun. Housewives began to find wares to haggle about, and schools returned to normal. Even the local Government now formed a National Congress of all constituted bodies to prepare the way for a National Assembly to consider plans for a new Constitution. But everyone now was a little wiser.

The progress of the war elsewhere was followed intimately and when at last Germany surrendered in May 1945 Malta went mad with rejoicing. Now the lights came back, and conscripts returned to civvies.

But it could not be said that Malta was going back to her pre-war days. For social, economic and political patterns had changed, and everyone knew that the country would never be the same again.

CHAPTER XII

POST-WAR SOCIAL AND POLITICAL EVOLVEMENT

It was now definitely all over and the time had come for sober reflection. There were 145 years of occupation to be reviewed, during which Malta had sustained a social upheaval and a bloodless revolution as complete as any in history. It was very British in character, and retaining a semblance of constitutional genesis and democratic execution. But still failing to produce any solid patterns for the future. When the last clamour of war and victories had died down, and one was ready to forget the British brand of democracy that had often advanced in sudden painful jerks, on occasions also going into reverse, it was time to see what had really been achieved.

There was now indeed less ignorance in Malta, and the way had also been paved for less squalor and poverty. The University had achieved a standard and reptuation which were second to none and was all set to continue producing a bigger crop of successful men and women without any having to resort to patronage which many years back might have been the door to any career. Unskilled men who had throughout the crisis and war worked at the dockyard or in the serviees had now emerged as skilled in some trade or more. Farmers who had always used wooden ploughs for their fields and treaded out the corn with a cow or mule, were now aware of harvesters, tractors and similar powered tools. But maybe the biggest change had come in the way of self-recognition which led to a better understanding of the British people as distinct from their government.

The Maltese had often considered the British to be cold and reserved. Seen against the local characteristic of selecting friends by opening arms to every one, this had always run counter to the belief that the British would open theirs to no one until they were certain that friendship would develop. Now it could be realised how they must have felt about Maltese exuberance being too much for them. With a dearth of topics for communication being more due to the fact that it had been so easy for them to get onto dangerous ground with talk about poverty, politics and religion. These had once been the only external impressions of the British on Malta. And there had also been their incomparable humour which the Maltese failed to understand. Notwithstanding the many occasions for dialogue, the two peoples had for a long time looked at each other across a wall of misconception. And it had to be the war to raze that wall to the ground and bring them together for the change that had occurred.

It wasn't a change in what was traditional. But in the future that everyone was looking for. The Maltese had always started day with tea or coffee but this had now become breakfast. Those who had been in the services or worked close to them had now assumed manners, accent, turns of phrase and even the way of dress to conform with the social coloration they had come to know. And this somehow fitted the quickly developing English background. Streets, houses, cinemas, shops and similar establishments were all carrying English names. Some parents had even taken to the habit of talking to their young in English. Not through some deference to the Maltese language but because that of English was riding high and had even become the predominant subject in schools, as it had remained the official way of expression in the civil service. Where in normal conversation no Maltese translations or equivalent were found then English words which came easier to the tongue were used and these were eventually to go into the Maltese vocabulary where they were to stay.

This encroachment of British characteristics into the

realms of Maltese life was not, however, restricted to this. There were the thousands of books in English that were brought into the island by the services and their libraries. Novels, thrillers and even something more serious were still finding avid readers to be transported to a fantasy of a Britain and her customs they had only just come to know. What the books did not do there were the newspapers to do it. Now the Maltese were no longer being scandalized by the gamier aspects of sex and bigamy in the *News of the World*. They read Cassandra in the *Daily Mirror* where they also followed *Jane*. All the London newspapers were finding a steady readership in Malta, and many of them were soon looking for Maltese correspondents as if to produce a *quid pro quo*. It was at this time that there was generated the first Maltese support for British football which was to develop into the fantastic fever still existing in Malta to-day.

The only discordant note in an otherwise benevolent aura came from a handful of Maltese who had settled in Soho where they might have shed the wrong opinion about Malta. But then so might have done to their country some shibboleths of the British garrison in Malta. Odds were now even and forgotten. Anyway, all this was more in the way of a sideline. There were now more important things in the offing making those times momentous in that they could make or break the new nation being conceived.

There was therefore little or no time for trivialities. There began to be fewer people watching fleet movements in Grand Harbour. And those who did were more interested in the clearance operations being carried out on wrecks than in the new warships that were often in port. The raising of the tanker *Ohio* attracted more attention than the new aircraft carrier *Ocean*. And even the latest battleship *Duke of York* failed to draw the same interest as the raising of the sunken *Pampas* and *Talabot*. To the new generation all this meant nothing. But to the elders it brought back memories of past history and gave impetus to the more important deliberations that had to be made concerning the new one.

None was in doubt that there was a future to look forward to. But it had all been sounding like politics which had suddenly become a hobby for some, while to others it was still all greek. At least where it concerned the British connection. There had also been much ground covered by trade unions, now no longer the weak and decrepit groups of bygone days. The workers had rallied in their thousands behind their leaders clamouring for rights and even resorting to strikes. And nobody had stopped them since this was another factor in their emancipation in a field which Britain had pioneered. If any confirmation was required it came in 1945 when the Colonial administration promulgated the Trade Unions and Trade Disputes Ordinance. This legalised trade unions and their endeavours, thus bridging social and political chasms. On the political front the promised Constitution was heralded by the arrival of Sir Harold MacMichael in 1946. He was a distinguished retired administrator in the Middle East now roped in by the British Government to consult the National Assembly and formulate proposals for constitutional reform. More important were his recommendations for a Legislative Assembly of forty members to be elected on a system of proportional representation, leaving out completely the constitution of an upper house which had featured before. There was however an innovation with the giving of the vote to women for the first time. The stage was then all set and the rest was left to the political parties that were to contest this first post-war election.

After its pre-war debacle the Nationalist Party drew more curiosity than interest. No doubt making many remember its pro-Italian attitude of the thirties and raising speculations on its role in the new times. Particularly that there was to lead it the same veteran pro-Italian Dr Enrico Mizzi just returned from his internment in Uganda. It was however expected to see Miss Mabel Strickland filling the breach for her late father and lead what was now called the Progressive Constitutional Party. But the new horse was the Malta Labour Party. Not with the old set-up of the twenties. But a well organized ensemble with a wide trade union backing, and which had already spread quickly all over the island. It was led by the same Dr Paul Boffa. Two small newly emerged parties made no impact and there were no bets on the results of the election that followed in

172

September 1947. It had indeed by then become a foregone conclusion that the Malta Labour Party would win. And so it did, with 24 seats. The Nationalists were runners up with seven.

It was all well and good for the new Government to think in terms of reconstruction, maintaining employment, enacting industrial legislation and improving social services. All were badly needed by a barren Malta. But there was also awareness of the need to diversify and generate new economic activity. To function in time when Britain might be compelled to cut her defence spending.

To those who had counted on an everlasting British connection this seemed a gross unlikelihood. But a hint might have been taken in 1945 when the first British sent expert Sir William Woods gave advice on finance and future economical development. There were others to follow with little or no result. But all pointing at British thinking that there will come a time when the base at Malta would not be sustained.

For those who were prone to notice them British inclinations towards this end could be interpreted from what was going on in the Mediterranean. Most particularly in the eastern part where soon after the end of hostilities the situation was not very peaceful and British troops were used to police troubled areas under a United Nations mandate. Such as in Greece and Palastine. Now that the mandate had ended these troops were being slowly withdrawn. Britain had also withdrawn from India, and this might have given the idea that it would release more naval forces for the Mediterranean and Malta. But the strategists were now decreeing that the Royal Navy's new main task lay more and more in the North Atlantic to guard resupply routes from America to Europe and watching over a new powerful Soviet fleet based in the Sea of Murmansk. So the naval stations still held in the Mediterranean had become superfluous to strategic planning.

What the disappointed people could not understand, however, was that while Britain was thus gradually removing her naval forces from the Mediterranea, the United States and Russia were introducing theirs. There was also the formation of the North Atlantic Treaty

Organisation in April 1949 with one of its three commands CINCSOUTH being located at Naples to control the Mediterranean.

There were hopes that the naval rundown to which Britain now seemed to be irrevocably committed would not concern Malta. The niceties of close friendship, and the development of the bond through the years were suddenly all being recalled. As well as the sacrifices of the battle fought together only a few years back. All being put at the other end of the scale to weigh down positive deliberations. Hopes were strenghtened when it became known that Princess Elizabeth intended flying to Malta for Christmas to join Prince Philip who was in command of the frigate *Chequers*. At the same time that his uncle Lord Mountbatten was was also in Malta as Flag Officer of the 1st Cruiser Squadron. Lord Mountbatten was back in Malta after an absence of ten years. He had found his old residence Casa Medina had been converted into flats so he had to resort to a derelict ruin once called Villa Guardamangia. But under the directions of Lady Edwina this was soon turned into a modest house. Not by any standard to be compared to the great family estate Broadlands in Hampshire, but it was just what they wanted. Comfortable enough as a residence where they could entertain. And close enough to Mountbatten's off-duty recreations of polo, sailing and aqualung skin-diving. It was there that Princess Elizabeth was to stay, and it all seemed like a royal family reunion.

Yet, before this came to happen there was the feared bombshell. Dockyard workers began to be laid off.

It was bad in itself. But was even worse coming as it did when the island was still finding her feet. There were immediate reactions and protests and the Maltese government went all out to negotiate a reversal of the British decision. But even here there was disagreement between the Prime Minister and Mr Dom Mintoff, the Minister of Public Works and Reconstruction on the way the negotiations were to be handled. The result was a split, with the majority of the Malta Labour Party supporting Mr Mintoff, who assumed the leadership when the Prime Minister resigned to form his own Malta Workers' Party.

This was the same Dom Mintoff who had won a Rhodes scholarship in 1939, and had been described by Sir Charles Bonham Carter, the Governor at the time as being of a strong character and personality and that he was likely to take an interest in the government of his country. Indeed at the age of 33 he was already a successful architect and civil engineer, as well as a very active politician in the fold of the Malta Labour Party. His assumption of its leadership came like a clarion call to clear the decks for the political fight that seemed imminent. However, in the election that followed shortly after in 1950, the electorate voted the Nationalist Party into power, and Dr Enrico Mizzi became Prime Minister. This raised different speculation. Not as much how he would tackle the crisis as to what attitude he would take since there had been nothing to indicate he might have changed from his pro-Italian leaning. Still, he kept everyone guessing, for ironically enough he died three months after taking office. And he was succeeded by Dr George Borg Olivier.

Strangely enough, although British attitude was one of disarmament there were flashes that ran counter to it. While Maltese regular regiments were allowed to dwindle down to unoperational strength, there were started territorial elements composed of part-timers who were having week-end camps on full military footing. Many ex-officers and other ranks from the regiments that had emerged victorious from the ordeal of the last war made more than a hobby of this training. It gave them a chance to continue in the kind of life they had known. A life of promptness and punctuality, smartness and correct forms of behaviour in the best of British tradition. Coming to think of it these must have been factors to be misinterpreted by people with different cultural backgrounds that this might have sometimes led to British/Maltese friction. But those who understood the British character and systems of organisation rarely if ever had grounds of complaint.

And these systems of organisation were soon to be induced in the local population through the Civil Defence Corps which came into being in 1951. This was a British financed, disciplined and uniformed body built round a handful of picked officers, mostly seconded from the

Malta Civil Service, and commanded by Lt. Colonel J.V. Abela, OBE, a retired officer from the Royal Malta Artillery. All of them being trained in the UK not only in defence against modern methods of warfare, but also in organisation and population control in peacetime catastrophes. And this knowledge they imparted to the thousands who rallied around them. But perhaps their achievements could be better assessed by the way they set about in preparing Malta for any eventual emergency. An intricate set up of an underground central headquarters, spacious enough and fitted to house the government of the day, eight flour mills to feed a besieged population and a shelter link up scheme which could literally transfer towns and villages underground. All this was dug in solid rock, and made out to resist the rigous of a nuclear attack which in those days was already a threat.

By now, a part-time territorial force was set up. Maltese sandhurst-trained regular army officers also continued to make headway in both British and Maltese regiments. A few of them even reached the rank of Brigadier.

It was at this time too that there was a spurt in industrial legislation. And every bit that was being promulgated began to be modelled on corresponding laws in the United Kingdom. The General Workers' Union, not being happy with the prevailing situation resorted to call for help from the Trade Union Council of Great Britain in May 1951, which brought none other than Mr Arthur Deakin to survey the situation. So what the Maltese came to know in labour relations which are still practised to-day, can be said to have been modelled on the British.

Maybe most of this lost significance in the timely drive for constitutional emancipation of the fifties. It fell now to Dr Borg Olivier to start the ball rolling and open discussions with the British Government, who somehow seemed to be anxious to end direct colonial rule of Malta which did not fit in their intentions for the Mediterranean. While the discussions started Dr Borg Olivier had also to see to strengthening his position in government since he did not command a working majority, and it took him two further elections and a coalition with Dr Boffa to do it. In the meantime the American 6th Fleet and the Russians had strengthened their presence in the Mediterranean, while there was also another NATO command CINAMED established at Malta. It had also by now become obvious that any withholding of discharges would be only a temporary solution. There had therefore to be an endeavour for a change in Malta's constitutional status.

Dr Borg Olivier's proposal in this respect was for the transfer of responsibility for Malta from the Colonial to the Commonwealth Relations Office. This was tantamount to requesting Dominion status and the British Government rejected the proposal. Instead it suggested to have Maltese affairs removed from the Colonial to the Home Office. This was rejected by the Maltese leaders. There was a deadlock, but neither side was inclined to have the matter closed. In an attempt to keep it open, in 1954 the British Government suggested all party talks to be held in London, and in 1955 on being returned to power in another election Dom Mintoff accepted the suggestion on assuming office. His request now was to have Malta integrated with the United Kingdom, but retaining her local autonomy and Parliament, with power to legislate on all matters other than defence and external affairs. It would as such be represented in the House of Commons at Westminster by no fewer than three Members to be elected in accordance with United Kingdom electoral laws.

In some quarters this might have been seen as a rather tall order and even playing for high stakes. But on sober reflection it represented the answer to many unasked questions. Hearts still smarting from a terrible war but warm from the close association that had developed with the British people as a result were still languishing for something closer to Britain than a mere self-governing constitution. And what could have been closer than integration? And the British Parliament's reaction to this proposal was generally sympathetic. The British Prime Minister, Sir Anthony Eden, did not take long to act on it. In July 1955 he announced the convening of a Round Table Conference to consist of all political parties at Westminster to consider the propsal. In the meantime the British Government agreed to assume responsibility to help Malta diversify her economy. From one dependent on war and crisis to another built on industrialization.

It was a feather in Dom Mintoff's cap. But to many it was still unbelievable. None could believe that Britain would integrate with a former colony. However, the conference was convened under the chairmanship of the Lord Chancellor, Lord Kilmuir. Seventeen members were present including Lord Atlee, Mr Aneurin Bevan and Mr Clement Davies. As if to emphasise this was not a dream twelve plenary sessions were held in London, and another three in Malta, and all seemed to be going well. There didn't even appear to be any fears from any subversive voices that might have interfered on the many previous occasions to torpedo some developing improvement in British/Maltese relations. That seemed to be all past and gone. Indeed the Conference Report was published in December 1955 and the conclusion was that Maltese representation at Westminster was practicable and reasonable. It was therefore to be recommended for acceptance by Her Majesty's Government and Parliament, if it were also accepted by the people of Malta.

What a question! As if it wasn't the majority of the people who had realised this was the answer to the country's aspirations. It was expected that there would be those who would obstruct the issue. Like those who had always thought of Malta as belonging elsewhere. But those were now in a minority. And Mintoff told his people that integration seemed to be in the bag. However, enthusiasts who reasoned this way must have forgotten the Church. As always it was a force to be contended with. And although not openly hostile to the plan it had its misgivings about having Malta forming part of a Protestant country. However premature, a referendum was to be held and there was already talk of a boycott. Still, 152,583 Maltese were asked to vote on 11th and 12th February, 1956 to express their wish or otherwise for the proposed integration. 67,607 voted in favour while 20,177 voted against. After considering 2,559 invalid votes it emerged that 62,240 had boycotted the poll.

Those opposed to integration lost no time in expressing themselves for the result not having produced a clear cut majority for the proposal. And the British Government shared their view. But the matter wasn't dropped. It was decided that the Maltese electors were to be given another opportunity to pronounce themselves on the matter at the next General Election. In the meantime Sir Anthony Eden announced after a debate in the House of Commons, that the British Government would have a Bill drafted in two parts. The first to contain a new Constitution for Malta, the second to deal with Maltese representation at Westminster.

Was he after all having second thoughts about the rigid definition of Malta's disappearing strategic value? It is not known. But only a few weeks later, on 26th July, 1956 there was the bombshell of Colonel Nasser of Egypt announcing the nationalisation of the Suez Canal. This came after agreement had been reached to the contrary and British troops were withdrawn from there a month before. A crisis erupted and Britain and France began to put pressure on Nasser to keep the canal open as an international waterway. But he was adamant. So they began to plan an assault which was to be launched on 15th September. It was no joke, and before Malta knew what was happening the Mediterranean fleet was back in her harbours. 100 warships and transports which made those days so reminescent of the invasion of Sicily. Aircraft taking part in the assault were to be shared by Maltese and Cypriot airfields.

Momentarily good counsel seemed to prevail and with the hope of a peaceful settlement the operation was postponed. But Nasser now began to receive Russian military experts and advisers which endangered the situation. To complicate matters further on 29th October Israeli forces attacked Egypt. So Britain and France decided to act. They both vetoed last resolutions by America and Russia in the United Nations in an attempt to avert war, and on the same day they launched the assault.

Now bombers from Malta attacked Egyptian airfields, while the 100 ship armada left to attack Port Said. The island was back to her offensive fortress role as if to dispel any belief in what the strategists had said seven years before that it had become superfluous as a base. One would have imagined that this might have strengthened the case for integration which continued to be discussed with fluctuating fortunes. But there was soon to be the surprise packet in the form of Mr Duncan Sandys running to Malta with the oracle that the island would still no longer be in the very centre of the European battle area in any future war. Therefore what further cuts were envisaged in Defence expenditure were to affect her dockyard.

The anxiety was now real, widespread and justified, for the Dockyard provided bread and butter for over 13,000 regular workers, and as Mr Lennox-Boyd, the Secretary of State for the Colonies himself said, "had always been the core of Malta". The Maltese government gave priority to have a guarantee of alternative employment if the dockyard were to close down. This was not given. The only alternative offered by Lennox-Boyd to avert the threatened deadlock was to have a five year trial run for Maltese economy to approximaet that of the United Kingdom with a grant of £25,000,000 spread over the period, and for integration to be held in abeyance until then. Obligation to help in case of mass unemployment was conditioned to this rising above the British level in consequence of Defence cuts. But this was not accepted.

The integration idea was killed, and the Maltese Labour government now raised the cry of independence. This had the support of the Nationalist Party in opposition which had combated Integration, and a resolution threatening severance of the link with Britain was passed in the House of Representatives unanimously and with acclamation.

More than a deadlock the situation had brought a constitutional crisis, and in the first part of the new year 1958 relations between the two countries became more tense. After Dom Mintoff tendered his resignation and that of his Cabinet on 24th April, 1958, trouble loomed ahead. The General Workers' Union staged a strike as a national protest. But this generated into rioting. There were pitched battles between rioters and the police in several localities, accompanied by acts of arson and pillage. The Governor, Sir Robert Laycock dissolved the Legislative Assembly and assumed powers to maintain law and order.

A further attempt to initiate fresh discussions was made by Mr Lennox-Boyd in November 1958 when it was thought matters had calmed down. But irrespective of what talks were carried out with the leaders of the Political parties there was no solution to the crisis. So on 5th January, 1959 the British Government repealed the 1947 Constitution and Malta was back to colonial rule.

CHAPTER XIII

ALTERNATIVE OF INDEPENDENCE

The initial reaction to the withdrawal of the Constitution was a general blaze of anger and a great upsurge of feeling to fight back. But then in the ominous days that followed, unbelievably beautiful days belonging more to summer than a wintry January, the lurking uncertainty gave in to a stronger than ever conviction to hasten the process of independence. It was now being seen like a bridge that had to be crossed. A bridge which was resting on two overarching themes: the diversification that had now become a must, and the tawdry impending rundown of British forces. More than mere themes these were now being seen as two important factors that had to be worked out together if a balance were to be maintained.

It was still felt, however, that there should have been something done in the way of an appreciation of independence, for which previous history had left Malta poorly prepared. And Dom Mintoff might have had this in mind when he suggested that independence should not come before 1962. Truly enough, the Colonial Administration now under the new Governor Sir Guy Grantham, who had become the first Naval Officer to administer Malta since Sir Alexander Ball had died in 1809, produced a five year plan. This envisaged the development of industry, tourism and agriculture, and it was estimated to cost £32,250,000. Of this the British Government was providing £22,000,000 in the form of grants and loans.

This was a step in the right direction. But it was only showing one side of the coin. There was on the other and popular side the inability to accept the realities of the British situation. In a more than ever imperfect world, and more particularly one that was again engaged in an armaments race the sentimental part of the people could still not understand and much less believe in the British decline. Since 1945 British defence budgets had been slashed year after year, and the Royal Navy which was Malta's main money earner had already become a shadow of its former self. Now there was a further drastic cut when the Malta Dockyard was closed down. Admittedly some energetic endeavours enticed the private Welsh firm of C.H. Bailey & Co. to take the yard over as a commercial enterprise and jobs were saved. But there was still something that died with this changeover. It became obvious that this was the beginning of the end.

It was not long when Manoel Island which had for ages housed the submarines whose names are still remembered for their exploits, was taken over to be turned into a yacht marina; anti-aircraft batteries which had gone down into the pages of history began being turned into farms. Forts which for centuries had housed only troops and guns were now being turned for different use. Marsa which since time immemorial was connected with the military now began to take the first factories of an industrial estae. The fort was being dismantled.

In contrast NATO had installed one of the latest types of radar at Madlena on the nothern side of the island while it established its headquarters in a magnificent building which had risen from war dust in Floriana. On this building there now began to fly the flags of France, Greece, Italy, Turkey and the United States of America, as well as the Union Jack which continued to be hauled down for ever at one shore establishment after another. It seemed as if while Britain was running down her base NATO was building hers. Even Grand Harbour was now hosting more elements of the Italian, Greek and United States navies than British warships in connection with some NATO exercise. But to become more prominent in harbour there were now the big liners which were often calling to pick up thousands of emigrants for Australia and Canada. It had been anticipated by every expert that the island could not absorb all the services redundancies with the upcoming generation in the forthcoming independent set-up. So mass emigration was being encouraged. The pity of it all was that men who had entered the war without any particular skill had emerged out of it proficient in some trade or more. And this had inflated the skilled force for which there was certainly no immediate need. The alternative for these men was emigration, with the resulting drain of skilled people that were bound to be needed in the new Malta all were aspiring for.

The ideal arrangement would have been to slow the rundown and hasten independence. But what could one do with a Colonial Administration? There was a ray of light, however, in July 1960 when a constitutional commission was set up under Sir Hilary Blood to formulate proposals for the return of self-government. Six months later it published its report recommending a self-governing constitution without any reserved matters, making it encumbent on a Maltese government to consult the British on certain matters. But who cared? The new constitution was only going to be a means for independence, the drive for which was already gathering momentum. Blood's report was accepted and an election was set down for 1962. It was obvious that this was going to be a determining election with whoever gaining power being expected to transact the details of independence. Because of this it was hotly contested, but in the process the Malta Labour Party clashed with the Church for alleged political interference. And as had happened in 1930 with Lord Strickland the Church again placed the Labour Party executive under interdiction. Notwithstanding this the party won 16 seats. But the Nationalists won 25 and the election. The remaining seats went to three smaller parties. Now Dr Borg Olivier's first job was to make a formal request to the British Government to give Malta her independence in 1964.

This might have given the idea that all was well and Malta had only to wait the better times. But arguing in this way would not be taking into consideration the 160 years that the island had gone through under British rule. Never during those years were she required to deal or handle matters that were predominantly foreign since there had been little or no export activity. There had never been the factories and similar enterprises that were sprouting up now all requiring knowledge and know-how of markets and connected business. It follows that in those years of occupation there had never been any place or impetus for the skill of management. And it was only now that this art was added to the university curriculum. This explains why some of the new industries were having their first troubles. The one and only big industry during most years of the occupation had been the dockyard. Even this, now that it had been transferred lock, stock and barrel to private enterprise was having difficulties. In its time as a naval arsenal it had never wanted for technicians, and deadlines had not been that important since there was no element of competition involved. But now with its being a commercial concern what deficiencies there had been began to emerge. After all the private owner had to go by a balance sheet which the Admiralty never needed to produce. In 1963 C.H. Bailey Ltd. backed out and the yard was taken over by a Council of administration who engaged Swan Hunter, a well known shipbuilding and repairing firm to manage it on a fixed fee basis. By now it had become apparent that in this and other endeavours the Maltese were going to take time to come to terms with the new situation.

Still, nothing of this impeded them to go ahead to the new coveted ideal. When the British Government called a conference in London to discuss independence all the Maltese political parties took part. But it is not proposed here to recount the full sequence of the contest of wits, of devious negotiations, of dashed hopes and final agreement thrashed out at this Conference. It will suffice to say that only the three small parties had some reservations on the issue. But both the Nationalists and the Malta Labour Party which between them represented 70% of the electorate, and had included independence in their electoral programmes agreed and were all out for it. So it was granted.

On the night of Sunday, 20th September, 1964 the Parade Ground at Floriana, a century old venue for military ceremonials and pageantry had never seen so many people.

185

Flanked by Lintorn Barracks on one side, now conspicuous by its silent emptiness as if to symbolize the era that was going out, and St Publius Church on the other, once wantonly razed to the ground by Nazi raiders, now reconstructed and illuminated to confirm the will of a nation that had risen again to a new future. Even the rain that had threatened throughout the day seemed to hold back that night, as if not wanting to spoil the colourful and significant occasion that was to follow.

Prince Philip was there, to present the instruments of independene to Dr Borg Olivier. Witnessed by Mr Duncan Sandys and a host of foreign high dignatories. But the protagonists on that occasion were the people present who could not help recalling what they knew or had learned from previous generations of what Malta had gone through under British rule. There had been the good and the bad, poverty and affluence, co-operation and misunderstandings. All to be reconciled now in a coherent whole to be judged. And the result of this judgement was there to be seen on everyone's face and indeed in the general attitude.

At midnight which brought in Monday, the 21st, the Maltese red and white flag was hoisted to replace the Union Jack that had been hauled down. And the ceremony ended in a burst of cheering. Then to be followed by a sudden suppressed silence as it had begun.

As the people found their way back home in the early hours of the morning, however, they could see the silent streets were already veiled in iridescence awaiting dawn. Notwithstanding the unstable weather it was a warm night, and all knew that on arrival home they would open windows to catch what breeze there might be. It wouldn't be long then when they would also see the pink line against the horizon in the east that would signify the beginning of dawn. There would then be the sound of the first traffic, and the movement of early risers. The pealing of bells from nearby churches would then herald the new day. And none of them had any doubt that it would be a new day in more ways than one.

*　　*　　*

It wasn't, however, going to be the end. The Defence Agreement entered into by the two countries made it encumbent on Britain to retain a presence in Malta and make use of certain military facilities. The Financial Agreement laid down the payment for the use of these facilities to the tune of £50 million, spread out over the ten year period. With three quarters of this money being in the way of a grant and the rest as a loan at current lending rates in the United Kingdom. There was also to be provided £1 million for restoration of what historical buildings had been occupied and now released by British forces. This meant that ties with Britain were far frm being severed, and Malta remained within the Commonwealth with the Queen as her head of state to be represented by Sir Maurice Dorman, now Governor General. To represent the British Government there was appointed a High Commissioner.

Under the provisions of the Defence Agreement the British Army retained two Battalions in Malta, whilst the Royal Air Force kept the airfield at Ta' Qali with some fighter squadrons and that of Luqa which since the 1956 Suez crisis served as a base for Shackleton, Nimrod and Canberra aircraft. The Royal Navy took over Hal Far air station, but the fleet became unrecognisable with only an escort squadron of frigates and one squadron of inshore minesweepers to show the white ensign. The British forces seemed to have all dropped into a euphoria of sleepy contentment in contrast with a Malta bustling with activity. In search of expert advice on industrialization there was the usual recourse to Britain to supply the right person to do it. This time it fell to Lord Robens to come over with guidance on building the first factories.

Now there was progress and there was an evident improvement with tourism. It is true that this sector was helped by a British imposition of a £50 limit on holiday spending outside the sterling area which made Britain tourists flock to Malta and Gibraltar but it appeared more as if the British people were reciprocating Malta's overture of friendship when they made the absolute majority of the 70,000 tourists that visited the island by 1966. There were also the hundreds of residents attracted by a scheme offering the island's amenities and Maltese hospitality. As well as an income tax of only sixpence in the pound which begot them the name of sixpenny settlers. They settled down and mixed; happy with what the island had to offer them, as the Maltese were happy with them.

How much had this business affected the island economically? And in what way would it benefit British/Maltese close relations which were now running fast towards conclusion in 1974? With the coming of the residents there were soon to be seen the rows of neat well gardened villas stretching along the coast or in unexpected areas which no Maltese would have ever chosen for habitation, all surrounded by oleanders and grape-vine. This meant immediate benefits in purchasing of land, construction wages, openings for servants and of course more architects' and lawyers' fees. But they soon became a specimen and a living example of how one could enjoy living away from it all. Not for the locals, but for the tourists, particularly those from their own countries and who spoke the same language. Those who arrived in brightly coloured shirts for some annual meeting or just to have fun. Whether they were snoeklers, or escapists in search of the sun they were bound to notice and take back with them the news of a Malta that had become the one haven of peace that had remained in the world. And the tourists were followed by businessmen and enterpreneurs, maybe not as much attracted by the peace aspect as by the financial incentives being offered for starting their business. All this was intended to create enough jobs to take in the thousands that were still in employment with the services but would become redundant at the end of the Defence agreement. They would then move into their new job, and the British would leave the island in 1974 as quietly as they had come into it.

But it was not to be. In 1967 the axe fell again when Britain again decided to curtail military expenditure, and this meant a premature rundown of services employees in Malta.

There were immediate protests, and this time the Maltese were not alone. British residents joined in, and so did the Governor-General. Dr Borg Olivier accused Britain of having infringed the concepts of the 1964 Defence agreement. Then he flew to London for discussions, as Maltese and British relations became strained. Again good counsel prevailed, and in order to allow more time for Malta to generate more jobs the British Government agreed to slow down the intended rundown. However, to safeguard their interests the British made it clear that the situation was being followed and should there not be the expected result in generating new jobs then they were reserving the right to re-open discussions and reconsder their decision. The Prime Minister agreed, and the situation began to return to normal. Even so, the talks had taken their time, and so did the process of development. Before one had time to judge about the last course of action there was 1971 rushing in, with the new election that was due. An election that had to be fought between the Nationalist Party and the Malta Labour Party who had already declared its intentions to strive for a neutral Malta free from any military involvement. This meant that a Labour government would eventually even do away with the limited British presence in the island. A crucial decision both for Maltese and British interests.

It was indeed a hard fought election. With an equal number of seats going to both parties until there was only the one odd seat to be decided which would produce the winner. Even here the votes were found to be almost equally divided with the issue having to be decided by a handful of votes. These tipped the scales for the Malta Labour Party.

But this still wasn't the end. Because of the close result and the important issues involved there was to be a recount. The air became very tense, and so much depended from the second count. Three candidates were still in the running. Two Nationalists and a Labourite, with a number of votes which could only produce one quota. It was decided that the recount be undertaken by one counter instead of the normal eight in a team. A hushed silence fell on the thousands in the counting hall as the sole counter was selected and went through all the votes that were to decide the election and the many important issues. Press and radio representatives watched, and followed that fantastic recount. Hearts throbbed and hopes fluctuated as the counting proceeded. All eyes were centred on the sole counter with his supervisor packing voting papers as they flew into the counting trays. And the same feelings must have prevailed with the thousands following the proceedings by radio since on the outcome hinged the destiny of the nation.

The end finally came. With the same handful of votes giving the quota to the Malta Labour Party and the advantage of one seat and a government.

CHAPTER XIV

COUNT DOWN TO THE END

The first days of the new decade of the seventies which was to witness political domination by the Malta Labour Party were momentous ones. Changes began falling into pattern. But what concerns this story is the British connection which was then suddenly being seen as having reached the evening of its days. Opinions differed, and this was made quite evident by the rival political factions. Which was without a doubt a healthy sign of the democratic element. But it had already been declared that the new government would be adopting a new policy of neutrality which would keep the island politically equidistant from the two super powers in the Mediterranean. It was also intended to rid Malta once and for all of the foreign military base and to have her assume a totally independent role in world affairs.

This obviously meant as well the end of the limited British military presence, and the ball was set rolling with the resignation of Sir Maurice Dorman as the last Governor-General. His place was filled on 3rd July, 1971 by a Maltese – Sir Anthony Mamo, who had been Attorney General and Chief Justice. Now he became the first Maltese Governor-General.

It immediately became evident that the new situation would have to consider also all sorts of imponderables. If the British were leaving who would then guarantee the island's defence in a world which was still producing potential agressors? Was the island's economy stable enough to lose in one go what income was being received for the use of the base? These were basic questions that called for an answer before the changeover being envisaged could take place. As it was, however, the need for these replies did not arise since it appeared that there had been no specific plan set down for an immediate cessation of the British connection. It was true that Dom Mintoff had declared that with the unexpected rundown of services employees in 1967 Britain had virtually infringed the concepts of her Financial and Defence agreements with Malta. This had also been said by the Nationalist government at the time. But to a British protest denying this and arguing that the agreements were binding up to 1974 the Maltese Prime Minister came back to say that both agreements would have to be radically revised if they were to continue and be respected.

This gave a breathing space to those who were interested in retaining the connection but there was also preoccupation in expecting a possible British stand. No doubt all were remembering the many declarations about Malta's decline in strategical value and a Britain still madly obsessed on running down her military forces. But by contrast to all this there was an immediate positive reaction to the Prime Minister's statement, and on 19th July, Lord Carrington the Minister of Defence and Lord Balniel the Minister of State flew to Malta for talks with Dom Mintoff on his request for the revision of the two agreements.

It wasn't of course as simple as that, and the new issues had overnight become a hot subject for discussion in the House of Commons. There was appointed an ad hoc Anglo-Maltese Parliamentary Group under the chairmanship of the conservative Patrick Wall to go into the matter. "As the Mediterranean South Coast and North Africa are potentially hostile," Wall said, "Malta was still of strategic importance. Maybe more to NATO than Britain."

NATO had by now automatically come under fire with the new government's decision to divest the island of foreign bases, and in August 1971, it left its headquarters in Malta and transferred to Naples. The American Sixth Fleet too which had been a frequent visitor, now stopped calling at Maltese ports.

When it was known that the Maltese Government had demanded some £30 million a year for the use of the base instead of the original £4.8 million, those who had hoped for some sort of reapproachment saw such hopes faiding out. Now even the most staunch optimists had to admit that the British era was very likely to end prematurely. On the other hand one might have argued that once the matter had resolved itself into one of financial bargaining there might be place for some compromise. But as days flew past with the British Government still studying what could be suggested as a counter offer hopes continued to fluctuate. Not only in Malta, but also elsewhere as the situation was being followed. The removal of a British base from Malta was no doubt welcomed in Libya who was already helping the island. But it would also dismantle a bulwark to Italy's southern confinities, deny a haven to the American Sixth Fleet, and could also entice overtures from Russia with her ever increasing fleet in the Mediterranean. But the real drama concerned the Maltese. And maybe to a lesser extent the British. The general thinking now was that apart from her latest protest Britain had not shown any inclinations to prolong her presence in Malta. Indeed what establishments being vacated with the rundown were being handed to the Maltese Government as if to hasten even more the dismantling that could be seen going on and everywhere. And what was handed over was being used for the new Malta that was being mounted. Auberge de Castille for more than a hundred years the exalted head-quarters of the British army had already been taken over to become the Prime Minister's office, while the fabulous Admiralty House which had housed a long line of Commanders-in-Chief was soon re-opened by government as a National Museum of Fine Arts. Forts and other military establishments were standing down and making way for local tenants. Every building that had contributed its share to the history of the British in Malta was going. Then as if to pose a conundrum there was the much expected British reply in the form of a counter offer amounting to some £8½ million for the continued use of British and NATO facilities.

It struck the people like a thunderbolt, raising arguments

and hopes which were soon dashed to the ground when it was known that this too had been rejected.

There were now more anxious and palpitating hearts. Never since the war had Malta witnessed such tense moments. As indeed Britain must have never confronted such a tenacious Malta in her long years of occupation. More than anything else one might have described the situation as a financial tug-of-war, and it was an open secret that Dom Mintoff's aim was to get sufficient money to allow him accelerate the pace of economic diversification to see him through to the day when the country will have to stand on her own feet without the need of a military base. The question was how much he could stick his neck out with a Britain now apparently extended to her utmost limit. Pressed as she was with problems which were certainly more serious than the Malta affair. She was now being slowly strangled by the national electric power cuts and the jobless were increasing by leaps and bounds. The coalminers had gone òn a prolonged strike and normal life was thrown into havoc. As if this were not enough there was a sense of alarm on the doubtful outcome of a debate in the Commons on whether the nation should join the European Common Market or not.

The only sense of despondency in Malta emanated from the possibility of having to spend a doubtful approaching Christmas. It was indeed just before Christmas that Lord Carrington expressed the wish to go again to Malta for further discussions. And on Christmas day Dom Mintoff gave his reply. There was no scope for further discussions, and there had to be a final decision. If no agreement was reached then British forces in Malta will no longer be tolerated after the end of the year. But his claim had been trimmed down to £18 million.

Britain was still not ready to pay that much, and on 29th December she decided to withdraw her forces from Malta. From his end Mintoff extended the evacuation date to 15th January. But what had before been a stretch of amicable discussion had now become a crisis.

*   *   *

Never in 170 years had there been such a rift in the

Anglo-Maltese camp. And this time it was accomapnied by a sort of ultimatum with a limit too close for comfort. The British Government found the situation intolerable too and decided to end the bickering once and for all. So it ws decided to evacuate Malta. From there onwards this had to be planned like a military operation, leaving nothing to chance, and to be carried smoothly and in time to avoid incidents. First on the list to leave were placed the dependents. There were 4,700 of them, all women and children, no doubt regretting to have to leave the island and more because it had to be in this way. None of them hid this fact, and some were even crying openly when they had to talk about it. But now there was no place for feelings and regrets. They were given enough time to pack and bid farewells. Then the airlift was to begin on 8th January, 1972.

Until then nothing moved. It seemed as if everyone who under normal circumstances would have had to say something was now struck dumb. It became evident that the Maltese Government's stand was no fluke, while British pull-out preparations that were started continued uninterruptedly. The people just watched and hoped. And when they could hold themselves no longer they resorted to prayer as the Church had directed them.

It was indeed from this direction that there came the move in an attempt to break the deadlock. On 8th January the first dependants were in the RAF part of Luqa airport awaiting embarkation on a Hercules aircraft. These were the expectant mothers who were allocated a Stork Special priority flight. On the civil part of the airport the last few of a queue of passengers had boarded a waiting BEA aeroplane. But the door remained open and the boarding steps in place as if the plane was waiting for someone else. Then out of the VIP sector of the terminal there emerged the diminutive Archbishop Sir Michael Gonzi, accompanied only by his chaplain and an airport official. With quick steps which gave the lie to his 86 years he crossed the tarmac to the waiting aircraft. No ceremonial, no fanfare, nothing. His arrival and departure had the looks of a secret mission. Indeed none but Dom Mintoff knew of his trip and its purpose. In a few hours he was in London. Two days later he met Mr Edward Heath, the British Prime Minister. The news of his mission broke out only when he was due to return. He was back in Malta on the 13th, this time to be besieged by a crowd of reporters all clamouring to know the latest knews. But all he said to them was that he had returned with some hope. Indeed what he meant was reflected later when it became known that the NATO council was discussing the Malta question, and, what was more important, that Britain was still ready to resume talks. The families airlift had by now been completed.

But the seriousness of the whole matter was not being hushed any longer and anxiety had spread to Italy who issued an invitation to the Maltese Prime Minister to pursue the matter further. This time Dom Mintoff obliged and flew to Rome on the 14th. There was a ray of hope everywhere now that it became obvious that things had began moving again. Feelings were strengthened when Mintoff returned on the 15th and with the time of the ultimatum now lapsed the British withdrawal continued as scheduled.

It had by now become obvious that Britain had reached the limit of her offering and was trying to prevail on NATO to increase hers and make the total into an acceptable figure. There was a hint of such an offer on 19th January and Dom Mintoff went again to Rome where he met Lord Carrington and Dr Joseph Luns, NATO's Secretary General. Talks were continued on the 28th and this time there were also Mr Edward Heath, the British Prime Minister and Signor Emilio Colombo of Italy, both no doubt trying to bring pressure on NATO. But to everyone's dismay on 8th February, the talks broke down.

The situation became bleak and nigh hopeless. There seemed nothing else to be done, and the parties directly concerned began to attend to their ultimate arrangements. The Maltese Government seeing to emergency services such as Air Traffic Control arrangements at the airport for which Egyptian Controllers were brought over to be familiarized with the equipment by the RAF controllers who had always run it. The British began to dismantle heavy equipment from their establishments. But this drama was hitting the people hardest. No matter how

196

much one tried to behave normally there was always the spectre looming ahead of what the immediate future would bring. Irrespective of one's feelings about the British connection it was evident for all to see that even the government who was taking all precautions should the British leave abruptly, was trying to reach an agreement. Obviously because this was the best way out of the impasse. If this did not materialize then thousands who were still earning their living with the British were at a loss of knowing what the morrow would bring.

For the young this was a new catastrophe that was threatening, and they might not have understood what it meant. But for the elders it was a poignant experience as if they had stepped back thirty years to the times of the war and siege they had gone through. The fluctuating situation from day to day recalled terrible pictures and painful experience of days when Malta was close to starvation and annihilation only to be saved in the nick of time by the valour and determination of British seamen and airmen who would risk life and all to break through the enemy blockade to get food and ammunition to the beleagured island. It was ironic to think that what differences existed were with the British Government. There was consolation in differentiating this from the British people with whom as government had often said there was no quarrel, and cherished relationships had never worn out. And in confirmation that this feeling was reciprocated there were published tourist statistics for 1971 when the dispute had started which showed tourist arrivals to have increased to 178,705, of which 108,935 were British.

One could find comfort from reminescences of August 1942 when Malta had only three weeks supplies of meagre rations, fuel and ammunition. And with no visible hopes of survival. Then there had been the prodigious convoy as if an answer to the island's prayers arriving miraculously on the feast day of Santa Maria which appropriately gave that name to the convoy for the annals of history. There had also been Italy's surrender coming again, as had the end of the Great Siege of 1565, on 8th September in 1943, the feast day of Our Lady of Victories. The people had prayed then. As indeed they were doing now.

There were the few who might have grown out of such beliefs. But the majority did not. And it was soon associating the daily bits of news coming in with the prayers that were daily rising from Maltese hearts. On 23rd February Britain suggested resumption of meetings at ministerial level ... the final offer in conjunction with NATO was raised to £14 million a year. Talks started at Malborough House in London on 5th March ... and this time Dr Luns joined in. Things were moving even if there was no sign of agreement.

Then it happened. Dom Mintoff flew to Rome for talks with Andreotti, the Italian Prime Minister and Aldo Moro, the Foreign Secretary. Sir Alex Douglas-Home, the British Foreign Secretary, who happened to be there for talks on the Common Market, joined in as well. Monsignor Gonzi too went to Rome where he had talks with Dr Luns and Vatican officials. There were news of the drafting of an agreement, but nothing materialised. In the meantime 1,500 members of the British services in Malta had already left, leaving only 2,000. Half of these were scheduled to leave in a week's time on 25th March. As everybody waited expectantly there were 1,650 services employees who were asked to stay at home because their establishments had closed down. Then on 20th March, the RAF Malta and the Naval Port Division held their farewell parades. It became a race against time.

On Friday, 24th March, 1972 there was a news flash. Agreement had been reached. The news electrified people into joyful demonstrations. It brought tears to the thousands who on that day, being the feast of Our Lady of Sorrows, were taking part in ceremonial processions which had been ordained by the Archbishop to be a special occasion for prayers for the solution of the crisis.

Whether it was fate or Providence that had willed it to be so, Dom Mintoff and Lord Carrington signed the historic agreement at Malborough House on 26th March, 1972. Britain was to maintain her forces in Malta until 31st March, 1979, paying in conjunction with NATO an anuual rent of £14 million. Furthermore, there was to be £1 million a year worth of Economic aid for 7 years. Italy and the United States were to provide £2,500,000 in economic aid from their part. Malta from her side was not to allow Warsaw Pact countries to make use of the island or any military facilities. Should the United States and NATO require such facilities for themselves they could negotiate for their use. Moreover, Britain and NATO were bound not to use Malta as a base against any Arab country.

*   *   *

Seven years were a long time. But they were expected to be packed with so many events that would make them look shorter. What British forces had left were soon returning with dependents to continue with their tour of duty. Now that the 1972 crisis was settled there was to be no more fuss or clamour. Things seemed to be back to normal. But were they? The rest of the world was certainly providing enough to occupy men's minds. Henry Kissinger was now in his final lap to bring a cease-fire accord in Vietnam. Spiralling oil prices had the classic ingredients for a fuel crisis, the Middle East was in turmoil, and Nixon was making history with the Watergate affair. Nevertheless the Malta situation, however tame, kept ticking. But any hopes there might have been of anything happening to change the course of events did not stand much chance of being realised. The Maltese Government was decided in having the base dismantled with all foreign forces evacuated as much as the British seemed to be determined to leave. The stage was being set for the grand finale which was to be one of the most decisive actions in the history of Malta and Britain – indeed, of all the Western World. And the time that was being taken to bing it about was only in the way of a count down.

It was to be expected to have those in the upper age bracket looking back over the years. And to start them there was Lord Louis Mountbatten arriving in Malta on 3rd March 1973. Shorn of the pomp and regalia he was known to have always liked to have around him, since this time he came only as President of the International Council of United World Colleges. But his presence was enough to take one thirty years back to the time when Malta and Britain fought in partnership against the common enemy and which fight had forged between them an everlasting bond. If any indication of this were wanted it was to be seen in the group of Maltese ex-servicemen who flocked to entertain Mountbatten. All of them having at some time served under him. Amongst them being also J. Micallef, who had like him survived the loss of the destroyer *Kelly* when she was sunk during the Nazi invasion of Crete in 1941. There was Anthony Zammit missing. He had wanted to emigrate to Australia after leaving the service, and having no money to pay for his passage had asked for help from Mountbatten. The admiral had obliged by giving him a passage on a cruiser of the Australian Navy. There were other occasions to be remembered of British Senior naval officers going to the help of Maltese ratings who served them. Too many to be recorded. But all of them leaving unforgettable impressions for posterity of the sense of attachment and comradeship that had particularly developed between the British Navy and Malta. There was also the aircraft carrier *Ark Royal* in harbour at the time to complement such memories. She was the third ship to carry this name. Her predecessor having been lost while ferrying fighter aircraft to Malta in November 1941.

However, such thinking pertained to war. And Malta was now building for peace and neutrality. Even the Territorials and the Civil Defence Corps had been disbanded, and in every effort and endeavour being made there was to be reflected the new nation in the offing. This was soon heralded by the issue of new bank notes which for the first time ever dropped the portrait of the Queen. Not in disrespect. But only in the course of events. In fact the Prime Minister was soon off for talks with Sir Alex Douglas-Home, the British Foreign and Commonwealth Secretary, in connection with a proposed European Security Conference and the European Economic Community. Soon after he also joined the Commonwealth Prime Ministers Conference in Canada. Then in the following year, on 13th December 1974, Malta became a republic within the Commonwealth and the British sovereign ceased to be the head of state. Now Sir Anthony Mamo, the Governor General, became the first President of

Malta.

The die was cast, and the Maltese were resigned to what had to be their lot. This had always been their outstanding and most excellent trait, their sense of resignation. Maltese laughter, sometimes mellow, sometimes acrid, seems to lighten the most tense situation. It saves them from the absurdities of life. It emanates of course from their deep faith continually being charged by prayer. This makes them strong to endure; and they come through. After any catastrophe they always rise up and build again out of the fragments. And this sense of resignation makes them accept things as they are. It had been like that in the beginning. It was so now, when the tune was to intensify efforts and achieve economic stability in time for the foreseeable day when the island will have to forge ahead on her own. They knew they will have to surmount the loss of some £30 million a year when the British leave, and this might have made them pause. After all there was still an election due which could effect the issue. But even this wasn't a situation to slack efforts that were being made to achieve economic stability. The dockyard, whch was as ever the biggest employer, was going all out to improve efficiency and introduce the new activity of ship-building; factories to increase production aiming at higher exports. And in this they were helped by the establishment of the first Maltese shipping line, Sea Malta. Tourism was expanded, also aided by the setting up of a national airline, Air Malta. There were positive results in this sector which attracted 272,516 visitors in 1974, and 334,519 in 1975 which was more than Malta's population. But the most significant and encouraging factor was that the majority of these visitors came from the United Kingdom. Many of them taking their time to look in awe at the high dome of the Church of Our Lady of Mount Carmel in Valletta taking shape. And noticing in the process how it was indeed higher than the belfry of the Anglican St Paul's Church only a hundred yards away. Little knowing of the whim that lay behind that story and which had persisted for ever a hundred years.

Maybe the British people were going to Malta because of her climate, or the historical background. It could have been also the English speaking population that attracted them. Or even because these visitors or their relatives had at some time served there. But the Maltese liked to think that this was more because of the bond of friendship that had been forged between the two peoples.

The 1976 election returned the same government to power, with no change in policy and objectives. There was only a change in the presidency after Sir Anthony Mamo retired, to be succeeded by Dr Anton Buttigieg, a poet and a former minister. Now the last sprint appertained to the British.

There were installations still to be dismantled. Facilities that had rendered sterling service for many years. Like Bighi Hospital, schools, barracks, airfields, clinics, power station, telephone exchanges and the intricate underground fuel storage depot with its 50 miles of inter-connected pipelines which could hold 56 million gallons of fuel. All of them being indicative milestones of the era that was coming to an end. But the most complicated operation concerned the rundown of the employees that were running them. Perhaps not as much difficult on the British side as on the Maltese Government who had to absorb most of them in another employment.

It was soon the turn of the Royal Air Force to dispose of the two operational squadrons that had been retained at RAF Luqa which had seen so much activity in the forties and then again in the 1956 Suez crisis. No. 203 Nimrod squadron was disbanded on 31st December, 1977. The other squadron, No. 13 (PR) composed of Canberras was to be retained a little longer. At least until October 1978 when it was expected to form the final link in the chain of RAF planes flying from Malta. That would bring to a close 60 unbroken years of RAF activity in the island which had been started by No. 267 (Seaplane) Squadron from RAF Kalafrana in August, 1918. It would also bring the two protagonists in the drama, Britain and Malta, within a few months of the expected Grand Finale.

These were months to be characterised by different ways of taking farewell. There was a spurt by military units to carry out some philantropic work as if they were all in earnest to leave a last good impression behind them.

Regimental bands played in towns and villages drawing appreciative and feeling crowds so reminescent of similar occasions throughout the years of occupation. Now, unwanted furniture, sports equipment and even gymnasia were handed over to private and deserving organisations. And in the speeches that normally accompanied such occasions there began to be noticed the quivers in the voices of those who delivered them. Concurrently one could not fail to sense rather than notice the movement that was going on as soldiers, sailors and airmen left for home with their dependants. This time they were going for keeps and there were tearful farewells, but nonetheless all were carried out unobtrusively as befitted the long years of friendship. In the same spirit too there was the British decision to hand intact to the Maltese Government what buildings and installations that had not yet been dismantled. These included the complete Air Traffic Control Tower and hangars at Luqa Airport, the fuel storage depots, the Royal Naval Hospital at Mtarfa, an 18 megawat power station and a refrigeration plant, as well as the one and only deep compression chamber in the island. All worth some £5 million in money, but much more in the use they were going to be for the new Malta.

It was also time for memories. And as if it was so planned, on 22nd February, 1979, Rear Admiral ONA Cecil, the last Commander of British Forces in Malta convened a meeting for his staff to discuss the final preparations for the evacuation at Palazzo D'Aurel in the picturesque village of Gudja. This was the same place used by Generals Dwight Eisenhower, Harold Alexander and Bernard Montgomery as well as Admiral Andrew Cunningham and Air Vice Marshal Sir Keith Park in July 1943 to plan and direct the invasion of Sicily. It was there that Eisenhower gave the word GO for the mighty allied armada that had assembled at Malta to swoop on Sicily, thus lifting the siege and opening the way to victory in the 1939/45 war. But Palazzo D'Aurel had a more significant meaning in that it had been the Headquarters of General Graham sent by Nelson to Malta on 9th December 1799, with two regiments from Minorca to form the spearhead of the force that was to relieve the island from the French.

Graham and his troops had arrived in Malta on the *Northumberland* and the *Culloden*, and had landed at Vittoriosa. It was at the same spot where the Maltese Government had now erected the monument commemorating the end of the British Military base. And it was there too that the final ceremony or Grand Finale was to take place on 31st March, 1979.

With every preparation falling in place now the days flew faster, more than ever before marked by hectic British activity all of which being weighed down with excitement and heavy feelings. The military part of Luqa airfield had closed down, and the RAF Officers' Mess had been turned into a reception centre to house foreign personalities coming to Malta for the festivities. However, in a storeroom there was found all the RAF mess silver worth thousands of pounds which somebody had cleared, signed for, but in the hectic excitement of the moment failed to send to the United Kingdom. Rear Admiral Cecil was by now being continually made to part with jackets, caps and other parts of his uniform by sections of the population; call them souvenir hunters if you will. But all with the same intention of having something more than memory of which to remember the times they were leaving behind. All such meaningful occurrances were of course being lost in the rush of celebrations that were being held which then culminated in a climax at the Farewell Concert held at the Manoel Theatre in Valletta which brought the British and Maltese communities together for the last time before parting ways. There were two bands for the occasion, and similarly two nationalities in the audience which packed the theatre. There were also two leaders to master the ceremony – the President of Malta and Rear Admiral Cecil, who between them made up the Parting Song which was the main number that evening, with the President writing the lyrics and the admiral composing the music. But the moving end came with the two men acting no doubt on behalf of the nations they represented, when they embraced, under a shower of flowers thrown by the audience which spontaneously broke out singing Auld Lang Syne. It was a fitting climax that notwithstanding everything must have been imprinted in the halls of history.

It was also an auspicuous prelude, indeed a starter to the final ceremony on 31st March, 1979. A bitterly cold day with a steady drizzle that persisted till the evening. But even this did not keep away the thousands who made it a point to be present. People of every class of age who ignored the inclement weather and stood for hours, their minds and senses absorbed in the speeches that were delivered and drawing power from the surging speakers' voices all forecasting the birth of a new Malta. Not without the burden of sacrifices, that will however eventually take the country into better times. It was a ceremony which offered the extremes of emotion, from gloom to ecstasy which reached its fulcrum in the lowering of the Union Jack marking the end of an era and the raising of the red and white Maltese flag to make the beginning of another that was immediately heralded by singing, fireworks and the pealing of church bells.

Then, when all the noises died down, the crowd too became suddenly quiet. Only eyes moved as they were lifted first towards the Flame that was lit and which was to be kept continuously alight. Then to the Maltese flag flying alone in the cold breeze as a symbol of days to come.

In that brief moment there were tears in many eyes. Of those who cried in joy for the new Malta. And of others, who cried as well, but did not knew for whom.

EPILOGUE

What did the future hold? This was the question on many a Maltese lip after the British had left. The Labour government of the day had to start almost from scratch and lay down policies to tackle new problems that were obviously arising. The country's reliance for economic help was soon being placed on a different set of nations. China, Russia and her satellite countries became new friends, while Libya, Italy and Algeria gave guarantees of security. This was seen to fit Malta's new policy of neutrality and non-alignment, now being also characterised by a decision to keep the island equidistant from the two super powers in the Mediterranean, Russia and the United States of America. It was however being feared by many that this new spirit of searching for friends could also lead to the progressive weakening and eventual end of all ties with Britain, and this was considered to be a bad omen for the future.

The new situation came to be emphasized by the sporadic occasions when the British press evoked the Maltese government's wrath which brought retaliation in the way of temporarily banishing British journalists from Malta. On at least one occasion Prime Minister Dom Mintoff also successfully sued one newspaper in a British court and obtained redress both in damages and an apology. But even now, the Maltese people decided to wait it out where British/Maltese relations were concerned. Even when there was the occasional resort to verbal vitriol against the British government, always accompanied by honeyed words for the people saying that the fight was not against them but against their government, the Maltese continued to wait as if like the Chinese they felt that everything comes through with waiting. There might also have been the instinctive ability to appreciate the dimensions of time in relation to seemingly urgent problems of the moment, and this must have generated the idea that after all, what was going on might have only been intended to test political will.

In the meantime the Maltese continued to read English newspapers and listen to the BBC; they became even more mad on British soccer and did not stop investing in Britain. They also continued to send their children to English schools. If this were to be taken as a testing time for the influence that had nurtured in the Maltese character during the 180 years of British occupation, then it became abundantly clear that this had become intrinsic in Maltese life itself, and nothing and no one was going to erase it, as long as it did not interfere with the sense of loyalty and patriotism towards one's country. Indeed by now many were considering the erupting litigations as only disputes between neighbours about where to put the garden fence. What bickerings there had been were all being looked upon as lovers' quarrels.

Nothing of this affected British tourists. They continued to flock to Malta in their thousands to enjoy the island's history, climate, and the warm hospitality of the good-natured Maltese. When there was a reduction from previous years, this was due to the worldwide recession which had also gripped their country in the beginning of the eighties. Even so, notwithstanding Maltese efforts to diversify and bring more tourists from the rest of Europe, British arrivals continued to top the lists, pumping more money into the economy, as if faithful to the decades of close friendship, and also aware that the revival of old ties was only waiting round the corner.

This came in 1986 when in the course of dredging a part of Grand Harbour for the berthing of ships carrying grain to newly constructed silos, it was found out there were too many unexploded bombs and wrecks for comfort on the sea bed. These were all remnants of the war. The Maltese government, still a Labour one and returned to power for the third consecutive time in 1981 now had Dr Carmelo Mifsud-Bonnici as Prime Minister. He had replaced Dom Mintoff in 1984. His government now asked Britain to clear the harbour of its war residue.

Opinions varied on the onus of responsibility for this cleaning, and another litigation was in the offing. But this was to be a test on the character of the British who even when fortunes were at their lowest ebb, were always outspoken in defence of what they considered to be right. Notwithstanding the usual bickerings it took only a round of talks and a hastener in the way of a Russian offer to do the cleaning. British divers were flown for the job, which was also followed by a financial grant. The matter was cleared. But it also brought a new wave of understanding of how friendship flourishes on realism. Granted her penchant for outworn ideas of the past, Britain was now being seen in her true light.

There were sighs of relief from all those who had waited which however exploded into a roar when the Maltese government agreed to a visit by the British frigate *HMS Brazen* in August 1986 to commemorate the epic of the Santa Maria Convoy on 15th August, 1942. As had happened on that memorable occasion when British and Maltese efforts had lifted the siege of Malta, the Maltese lined the rampant bastions around Grand Harbour to welcome the British warship. There were also the boats and launches carrying the more ardent well-wishers to accompany her to its berth.

Yes, it was a replica of the other fantastic occasion of 1st April, 1979. On that occasion the Maltese had saluted a departing friend. Now, seven years later, they were welcoming him back again.

With British/Maltese ties having thus been re-established, it was now time for Malta to switch back to her political and economic problems. The democratic process continued when the election of 1987 was not fought at the barricades, but in ballot-boxes. This time a Nationalist government was elected and Dr Eddie Fenech-Adami became the new Prime Minister. One could expect new trends and policies. But Malta was to retain her policy of non-alignment and ties of friendship with all nations. Far from being decadent and idle, relations between Britain and Malta now stood to be improved. The Maltese were again pulsating with life on 15th August, 1987 when on this year's commemoration of the Santa Maria Convoy they again hosted the Royal Navy, this time represented by the frigate *HMS Broadsword*. But the newly found links between the two nations were further symbolized when Dr Fenech-Adami and his Maltese delegation met Queen Elizabeth II during the Commonwealth leaders' conference at Vancouver in October 1987.

The Queen remembered with nostalgy her stays in Malta in bygone days. An invitation to visit the island made by the previous government was mentioned to her again. But it was then Dr V Tabone the Maltese Foreign Minister who rose to the occasion and speaking on behalf of the Maltese nation told Her Majesty that if she decided to come − all the Maltese people would welcome her gladly.

His words were full of meaning. Mostly that the ties that had for a 180 year era bound the two nations were still there. Nurtured as they had been by a common history, sacrifices and dangers shared as well as enemies overcome during a long, tempestous and historic partnership, which had only come to a friendly end a decade before.

They also sounded more like a herald to the beginning of a new era, based on friendship and understanding between the two nations.

APPENDIX A

BRITISH CIVIL COMMISSIONERS AND GOVERNORS

Civil Commissioners

Captain Alexander Ball, R.N.	1799 – 1801
Major-General Henry Pigot	1801
Sir Charles Cameron	1801 – 1802
Rear-Admiral Sir Alexander Ball, Bart.	1802 – 1809
Lieutenant-General Sir Hildebrand Oakes	1810 – 1813

Governors

Lieutenant-General Sir Thomas Maitland	1813 – 1824
General the Marquess of Hastings	1824 – 1826
Major-General Sir Frederic Ponsonby	1827 – 1836
Lieutenant-General Sir Henry Bouverie	1836 – 1843
Lieutenant-General Sir Patrick Stuart	1843 – 1847
The Right Honourable Richard More O'Ferrall	1847 – 1851
Major-General Sir William Reid	1851 – 1858
Lieutenant-General Sir John Gaspard le Merchant	1858 – 1864
Lieutenant-General Sir Henry Storks	1864 – 1867
General Sir Patrick Grant	1867 – 1872
General Sir Charles Van Straubenzee	1872 – 1878

General Sir Arthur Borton	1878 – 1884
General Sir Lintorn Simmons	1884 – 1888
Lieutenant-General Sir Henry Torrens	1888 – 1890
Lieutenant-General Sir Henry Smyth	1890 – 1893
General Sir Arthur Fremantle	1893 – 1899
Lieutenant-General Lord Grenfell	1899 – 1903
General Sir Mansfield Clarke, Bart.	1903 – 1907
Lieutenant-General Sir Henry Grant	1907 – 1909
General Sir Leslie Rundle	1909 – 1915
Field-Mashal Lord Methuen	1915 – 1919
Field-Marshal Viscount Plumer	1919 – 1924
General Sir Walter Congreve	1924 – 1927
General Sir John du Cane	1927 – 1931
General Sir David Campbell	1931 – 1936
General Sir Charles Bonham-Carter	1936 – 1940
Lieutenant-General Sir William Dobbie	1940 – 1942
Field-Marshal Viscount Gort	1943 – 1944
Lieutenant-General Sir Edmond Schreiber	1944 – 1946
Sir Francis (later Lord) Douglas	1946 – 1949
Sir Gerald Creasy	1949 – 1954
Major-General Sir Robert Laycock	1954 – 1959
Admiral Sir Guy Grantham	1959 – 1962
Sir Maurice Dorman	1962 – 1971

APPENDIX B

MALTESE
PRIME MINISTERS

Mr. Joseph Howard	1921 – 1923
Dr. Francesco Buhagiar	1923 – 1924
Sir Ugo Mifsud	1924 – 1927
Sir Gerald (later Lord) Strickland	1927 – 1932
Sir Ugo Mifsud	1932 – 1933
Dr. (later Sir) Paul Boffa	1947 – 1950
Dr. Enrico Mizzi	– 1950
Dr. George Borg-Olivier	1950 – 1955
Mr. Dominic Mintoff	1955 – 1958
Dr. George Borg-Olivier	1962 – 1971
Mr. Dominic Mintoff	1971 – 1984
Dr. Carmelo Mifsud-Bonnici	1984 – 1987
Dr. Eddie Fenech-Adami	1987 –

APPENDIX C

PRESIDENTS OF MALTA

Sir Anthony Mamo	1974–1976
Dr. Anthony Buttigieg	1976–1981
Miss Agatha Barbara	1982–1986
Mr. Paul Xuereb (Acting President)	1987–1989
Dr. Vincent Tabone	1989–1994
Dr. Ugo Mifsud Bonnici	1994–

BIBLIOGRAPHY

Attard, Joseph, *The Battle of Malta* (William Kimber, London, 1980)

Blouet, Brian, *The Story of Malta* (Faber & Faber London, 1972)

Brockman, Eric, *The Last Bastion* (Darton, Longman & Todd, London, 1961)

Elliott, Peter, *A Naval History of Malta, 1798 – 1979* (Patrick Stephens, London, 1980)

Hughes, Quentin, *Britain in the Mediterranean, and the Defence of her Naval Stations* (Penpaled Books, Liverpool, 1981)

Laferla, A.V., *British Malta* Books I & II (A.C. Aquilina & Co., Malta, 1938)

Lee, Hilda, *A Study in Constitutional and Strategic Development* (Progress Press, Malta)

Laspina, Rev. S., *Outlines of Maltese History* (A.C. Aquilina & Co., Malta)

Luke, Sir Harry, *Malta — An Account and an Appreciation* (G. Harrap, London, 1949)

Macmillan Allister, *Malta and Gibraltar* (W.H. & G. Collenbridge, London)

Middleton, Drew, *The British* (Secker & Warburg, London, 1957)

Times of Malta, Various dates

INDEX

219

Nurse of the Mediterranean, 106

Oakes, General Sir Hildebrand, 28, 32
Ocean, HMS, 171
O'Ferral, Sir Richard More, 67, App. A
Ohio, M/T, 159
Opera House, 77
Operation Hercules, 158
Order of St. John, 15, 18, 53
Order of St. Michael & St. George, 41
Orient (French flagship), 9
Ottoman, 5
Owen, Lieut.-Colonel, M.C., 75

Pace Forno, Father Gaetano, 73
Paladini, 4
Pampas, M/V, 157, 171
Panzavecchia, Monsignor, 118
Parata, 55
Parish priests, 91
Park, Air-Vice Marshal Sir Keith, 159, 163
Paul, Czar of Russia, 7, 18
Pedley, Mr. Fred, 74
Pennefeather, Lieut.-General, 74
Penrose, Admiral Charles, 42
Perellos, Grand Master, 3
Perez d'Alecio, Mateo, 4
Phoenicians, occupation of Malta, by, 3
Pigot, Major-General, 13
Pinto de Fonseca, Grand-Master, 4
Piracy, 49
Pitt, Prime Minister William, 6, 17
Pius VII, Pope, 40
Plasket, Mr. Richard, 42
Plumer, Field-Marshal Lord, 46, App. A
Ponsonby, Major-General Sir Frederick, 48, App. A
Portafoglio Maltese, 63
Portelli, Mr. Agostino, 69
Portugal, 5, 10
Pound, Admiral Sir Dudley, 151
Preti, Mattia, 4, 37
Prince of Wales, 120

Prince Philip, 174, 186
Princess (later Queen) Elizabeth, 174
Progress Press, 147
Progressive Constitutional Party, 172
Protestant Church, 163
Prussia, 21
Pullicino, Sir Philip, 136

Queen Anne, 3
Queen Elizabeth II, 209
Queen Elizabeth, HMS, 131

Ramillies, HMS, 132
Rawden, Mr. Francis, 44
Referendum, 178
Reid, Major-General Sir William, 72, App. A
Renaissance, 4
Renown, HMS, 132
Republic, 200
Repulse, HMS, 132
Revenge, HMS, 131
Rhineland, 134
Ricasoli, Fort, 76, 78
Rinella, Fort, 78
Risorgimento, 65, 80
Robeck, Admiral Sir John de, 121
Robens, Lord, 187
Rohan, de Polduc, Grandmaster, 5, 6
Romans, occupations of Malta, by, 3
Rommel, Field-Marshal Erwin, 151, 152
Rossignaud, Canon, 65, 68
Round Table Conference, 177/8
Royal Air Force, 125, 140, 147, 152, 167
Royal Air Force Malta Group, 110
Royal Commission, 128
Royal Malta Artillery, 88, 103, 138, 143
Royal Malta Fencible Artillery, 86
Royal Malta Fencible Regiment, 75, 77